Emma Goldman

ANARCHISM AND OTHER WRITINGS

ANARCHISM
AND OTHER WRITINGS

Emma Goldman

Reprinted by Frederick Ellis
8000 E. Girard, Suite 507
Denver CO 80231
ISBN 978-0-9793363-8-6

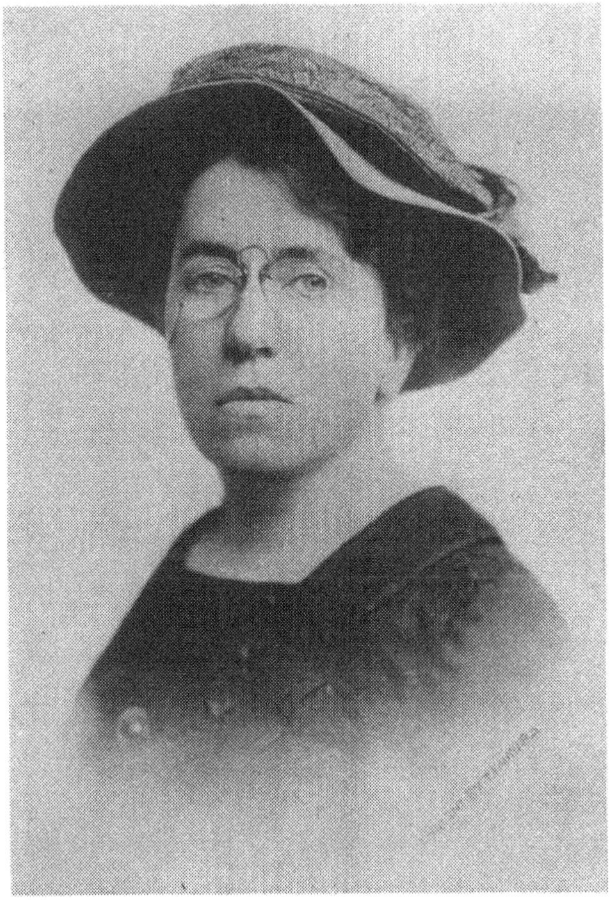

ANARCHISM
AND
OTHER WRITINGS

CONTENTS

EMMA GOLDMAN

Propagandism is not, as some suppose, a "trade,"
because nobody will follow a "trade" at which you
may work with the industry of a slave and die with
the reputation of a mendicant. The motives of any
persons to pursue such a profession must be different from those of trade, deeper than pride, and
stronger than interest.

GEORGE JACOB HOLYOAKE.

AMONG the men and women prominent in the public
life of America there are but few whose names are
mentioned as often as that of Emma Goldman. Yet
the real Emma Goldman is almost quite unknown.
The sensational press has surrounded her name with
so much misrepresentation and slander, it would seem
almost a miracle that, in spite of this web of calumny,
the truth breaks through and a better appreciation of
this much maligned idealist begins to manifest itself.
There is but little consolation in the fact that almost
every representative of a new idea has had to struggle
and suffer under similar difficulties. Is it of any
avail that a former president of a republic pays homage
at Osawatomie to the memory of John Brown? Or
that the president of another republic participates in
the unveiling of a statue in honor of Pierre Proudhon,
and holds up his life to the French nation as a model

worthy of enthusiastic emulation? Of what avail is all this when, at the same time, the *living* John Browns and Proudhons are being crucified? The honor and glory of a Mary Wollstonecraft or of a Louise Michel are not enhanced by the City Fathers of London or Paris naming a street after them—the living generation should be concerned with doing justice to the *living* Mary Wollstonecrafts and Louise Michels. Posterity assigns to men like Wendel Phillips and Lloyd Garrison the proper niche of honor in the temple of human emancipation; but it is the duty of their contemporaries to bring them due recognition and appreciation while they live.

The path of the propagandist of social justice is strewn with thorns. The powers of darkness and injustice exert all their might lest a ray of sunshine enter his cheerless life. Nay, even his comrades in the struggle—indeed, too often his most intimate friends—show but little understanding for the personality of the pioneer. Envy, sometimes growing to hatred, vanity and jealousy, obstruct his way and fill his heart with sadness. It requires an inflexible will and tremendous enthusiasm not to lose, under such conditions, all faith in the Cause. The representative of a revolutionizing idea stands between two fires: on the one hand, the persecution of the existing powers which hold him responsible for all acts resulting from social conditions; and, on the other, the lack of understanding on the part of his own followers who often judge all his activity from a narrow standpoint. Thus it happens that the agitator stands quite alone in the midst of the multitude surrounding him. Even his most intimate friends rarely understand how solitary and deserted he feels. That is the tragedy of the person prominent in the public eye.

The mist in which the name of Emma Goldman has so long been enveloped is gradually beginning to dissipate. Her energy in the furtherance of such an unpopular idea as Anarchism, her deep earnestness, her courage and abilities, find growing understanding and admiration.

The debt American intellectual growth owes to the revolutionary exiles has never been fully appreciated. The seed disseminated by them, though so little understood at the time, has brought a rich harvest. They have at all times held aloft the banner of liberty, thus impregnating the social vitality of the Nation. But very few have succeeded in preserving their European education and culture while at the same time assimilating themselves with American life. It is difficult for the average man to form an adequate conception what strength, energy, and perseverance are necessary to absorb the unfamiliar language, habits, and customs of a new country, without the loss of one's own personality.

Emma Goldman is one of the few who, while thoroughly preserving their individuality, have become an important factor in the social and intellectual atmosphere of America. The life she leads is rich in color, full of change and variety. She has risen to the topmost heights, and she has also tasted the bitter dregs of life.

Emma Goldman was born of Jewish parentage on the 27th day of June, 1869, in the Russian province of Kovno. Surely these parents never dreamed what unique position their child would some day occupy. Like all conservative parents they, too, were quite convinced that their daughter would marry a respectable citizen, bear him children, and round out her allotted years surrounded by a flock of grandchildren, a good, religious woman. As most parents, they had no inkling what a strange, impassioned spirit would take hold of the soul of their child, and carry it to the heights which separate generations in eternal struggle. They lived in a land and at a time when antagonism between parent and offspring was fated to find its most acute expression, irreconcilable hostility. In this tremendous struggle between fathers and sons —and especially between parents and daughters—there was no compromise, no weak yielding, no truce. The spirit of liberty, of progress—an idealism which knew no considerations and recognized no obstacles— drove the young generation out of the parental house and away from the hearth of the home. Just as this same spirit once drove out the revolutionary breeder of discontent, Jesus, and alienated him from his native traditions.

What rôle the Jewish race—notwithstanding all anti-Semitic calumnies the race of transcendental idealism—played in the struggle of the Old and the New will probably never be appreciated with complete impartiality and clarity. Only now we are beginning to perceive the tremendous debt we owe to Jewish idealists in the realm of science, art, and literature.

But very little is still known of the important part the sons and daughters of Israel have played in the revolutionary movement and, especially, in that of modern times.

The first years of her childhood Emma Goldman passed in a small, idyllic place in the German-Russian province of Kurland, where her father had charge of the government stage. At that time Kurland was thoroughly German; even the Russian bureaucracy of that Baltic province was recruited mostly from German *Junker*. German fairy tales and stories, rich in the miraculous deeds of the heroic knights of Kurland, wove their spell over the youthful mind. But the beautiful idyl was of short duration. Soon the soul of the growing child was overcast by the dark shadows of life. Already in her tenderest youth the seeds of rebellion and unrelenting hatred of oppression were to be planted in the heart of Emma Goldman. Early she learned to know the beauty of the State: she saw her father harassed by the Christian *chinovniks* and doubly persecuted as petty official and hated Jew. The brutality of forced conscription ever stood before her eyes: she beheld the young men, often the sole support of a large family, brutally dragged to the barracks to lead the miserable life of a soldier. She heard the weeping of the poor peasant women, and witnessed the shameful scenes of official venality which relieved the rich from military service at the expense of the poor. She was outraged by the terrible treatment to which the female servants were subjected: maltreated and exploited by their *barinyas,* they fell to the tender mercies of the regimental officers, who regarded them as their natural sexual prey. These girls, made pregnant by respectable gentlemen and driven out by their mistresses, often found refuge in the Goldman home. And the little girl, her heart palpitating with sympathy, would abstract coins from the parental drawer to clandestinely press the money into the hands of the unfortunate women. Thus Emma Goldman's most striking characteristic, her sympathy with the underdog, already became manifest in these early years.

At the age of seven little Emma was sent by her parents to her grandmother at Königsberg, the city of Immanuel Kant, in Eastern Prussia. Save for occasional interruptions, she remained there till her 13th birthday. The first years in these surroundings do not exactly belong to her happiest recollections. The grandmother, indeed, was very amiable, but the numerous aunts of the household were concerned more with the spirit of practical rather than pure reason, and the categoric imperative was applied all too frequently. The situation was changed when her parents migrated to Königsberg, and little Emma was relieved from her rôle of Cinderella. She now regularly attended public school and also enjoyed the advantages of private instruction, customary in middle-class life; French and music lessons played an important part in the curriculum. The future interpreter of Ibsen and Shaw was then a little German Gretchen, quite at home in the German atmosphere. Her special predilections in literature were the sentimental romances of Marlitt; she was a great admirer of the good Queen Louise, whom the bad Napoleon

Buonaparte treated with so marked a lack of knightly
chivalry. What might have been her future development had she remained in this milieu? Fate—or
was it economic necessity?—willed it otherwise. Her
parents decided to settle in St. Petersburg, the capital
of the Almighty Tsar, and there to embark in business. It was here that a great change took place
in the life of the young dreamer.

It was an eventful period—the year of 1882—
in which Emma Goldman, then in her 13th year,
arrived in St. Petersburg. A struggle for life and
death between the autocracy and the Russian intellectuals swept the country. Alexander II. had
fallen the previous year. Sophia Perovskaia, Zhe-
liabov, Grinevitzky, Rissakov, Kibalchitch, Michailov,
the heroic executors of the death sentence upon the
tyrant, had then entered the Walhalla of immortality.
Jessie Helfman, the only regicide whose life the
government had reluctantly spared because of preg-
nancy, followed the unnumbered Russian martyrs to
the étapes of Siberia. It was the most heroic period
in the great battle of emancipation, a battle for
freedom such as the world had never witnessed before. The names of the Nihilist martyrs were on
all lips, and thousands were enthusiastic to follow
their example. The whole *intelligenzia* of Russia
was filled with the *illegal* spirit: revolutionary senti-
ments penetrated into every home, from mansion to
hovel, impregnating the military, the *chinovniks,* factory workers, and peasants. The atmosphere pierced
the very casemates of the royal palace. New ideas
germinated in the youth. The difference of sex was

forgotten. Shoulder to shoulder fought the men and the women. The Russian woman! Who shall ever do justice or adequately portray her heroism and self-sacrifice, her loyalty and devotion? Holy, Turgeniev calls her in his great prose poem, *On the Threshold*.

It was inevitable that the young dreamer from Königsberg should be drawn into the maelstrom. To remain outside of the circle of free ideas meant a life of vegetation, of death. One need not wonder at the youthful age. Young enthusiasts were not then—and, fortunately, are not now—a rare phenomenon in Russia. The study of the Russian language soon brought young Emma Goldman in touch with revolutionary students and new ideas. The place of Marlitt was taken by Nekrassov and Tchernishevsky. The quondam admirer of the good Queen Louise became a glowing enthusiast of liberty, resolving, like thousands of others, to devote her life to the emancipation of the people.

The struggle of generations now took place in the Goldman family. The parents could not comprehend what interest their daughter could find in the new ideas, which they themselves considered fantastic utopias. They strove to persuade the young girl out of these chimeras, and daily repetition of soul-racking disputes was the result. Only in one member of the family did the young idealist find understanding—in her elder sister, Helene, with whom she later emigrated to America, and whose love and sympathy have never failed her. Even in the darkest hours of later persecution Emma Goldman always found a haven of refuge in the home of this loyal sister.

Emma Goldman finally resolved to achieve her independence. She saw hundreds of men and women sacrificing brilliant careers to go *v naród,* to the people. She followed their example. She became a factory worker; at first employed as a corset maker, and later in the manufacture of gloves. She was now 17 years of age and proud to earn her own living. Had she remained in Russia, she would have probably sooner or later shared the fate of thousands buried in the snows of Siberia. But a new chapter of life was to begin for her. Sister Helene decided to emigrate to America, where another sister had already made her home. Emma prevailed upon Helene to be allowed to join her, and together they departed for America, filled with the joyous hope of a great, free land, the glorious Republic.

America! What magic word. The yearning of the enslaved, the promised land of the oppressed, the goal of all longing for progress. Here man's ideals had found their fulfillment: no Tsar, no Cossack, no *chinovnik.* The Republic! Glorious synonym of equality, freedom, brotherhood.

Thus thought the two girls as they travelled, in the year 1886, from New York to Rochester. Soon, all too soon, disillusionment awaited them. The ideal conception of America was punctured already at Castle Garden, and soon burst like a soap bubble. Here Emma Goldman witnessed sights which reminded her of the terrible scenes of her childhood in Kurland. The brutality and humiliation the future citizens of the great Republic were subjected to on board ship, were repeated at Castle Garden by the officials of the democracy in a more savage and aggravating manner. And what bitter disappointment followed as the young idealist began to familiarize herself with the conditions in the new land! Instead of one Tsar, she found scores of them; the Cossack was replaced by the policeman with the heavy club, and instead of the Russian *chinovnik* there was the far more inhuman slave-driver of the factory.

Emma Goldman soon obtained work in the clothing establishment of the Garson Co. The wages amounted to two and a half dollars a week. At that time the factories were not provided with motor power, and the poor sewing girls had to drive the wheels by foot, from early morning till late at night. A terribly exhausting toil it was, without a ray of light, the drudgery of the long day passed in complete silence—the Russian custom of friendly conversation at work was not permissible in the free country. But the exploitation of the girls was not only economic; the poor wage workers were looked upon by their foremen and bosses as sexual commodities. If a girl resented the advances of her superiors," she would speedily find herself on the street as an undesirable element in the factory. There was never a lack of willing victims: the supply always exceeded the demand.

The horrible conditions were made still more

unbearable by the fearful dreariness of life in the small American city. The Puritan spirit suppresses the slightest manifestation of joy; a deadly dullness beclouds the soul; no intellectual inspiration, no thought exchange between congenial spirits is possible. Emma Goldman almost suffocated in this atmosphere. She, above all others, longed for ideal surroundings, for friendship and understanding, for the companionship of kindred minds. Mentally she still lived in Russia. Unfamiliar with the language and life of the country, she dwelt more in the past than in the present. It was at this period that she met a young man who spoke Russian. With great joy the acquaintance was cultivated. At last a person with whom she could converse, one who could help her bridge the dullness of the narrow existence. The friendship gradually ripened and finally culminated in marriage.

Emma Goldman, too, had to walk the sorrowful road of married life; she, too, had to learn from bitter experience that legal statutes signify dependence and self-effacement, especially for the woman. The marriage was no liberation from the Puritan dreariness of American life; indeed, it was rather aggravated by the loss of self-ownership. The characters of the young people differed too widely. A separation soon followed, and Emma Goldman went to New Haven, Conn. There she found employment in a factory, and her husband disappeared from her horizon. Two decades later she was fated to be unexpectedly reminded of him by the Federal authorities.

The revolutionists who were active in the Russian movement of the 80's were but little familiar with the social ideas then agitating western Europe and America. Their sole activity consisted in educating the people, their final goal the destruction of the autocracy. Socialism and Anarchism were terms hardly known even by name. Emma Goldman, too, was entirely unfamiliar with the significance of those ideals.

She arrived in America, as four years previously in Russia, at a period of great social and political unrest. The working people were in revolt against the terrible labor conditions; the eight-hour movement of the Knights of Labor was at its height, and throughout the country echoed the din of sanguine strife between strikers and police. The struggle culminated in the great strike against the Harvester Company of Chicago, the massacre of the strikers, and the judicial murder of the labor leaders, which followed upon the historic Haymarket bomb explosion. The Anarchists stood the martyr test of blood baptism. The apologists of capitalism vainly seek to justify the killing of Parsons, Spies, Lingg, Fischer, and Engel. Since the publication of Governor Altgeld's reasons for his liberation of the three incarcerated Haymarket Anarchists, no doubt is left that a fivefold legal murder had been committed in Chicago, in 1887.

Very few have grasped the significance of the Chicago martyrdom; least of all the ruling classes. By the destruction of a number of labor leaders they thought to stem the tide of a world-inspiring idea.

They failed to consider that from the blood of the martyrs grows the new seed, and that the frightful injustice will win new converts to the Cause.

The two most prominent representatives of the Anarchist idea in America, Voltairine de Cleyre and Emma Goldman—the one a native American, the other a Russian—have been converted, like numerous others, to the ideas of Anarchism by the judicial murder. Two women who had not known each other before, and who had received a widely different education, were through that murder united in one idea.

Like most working men and women of America, Emma Goldman followed the Chicago trial with great anxiety and excitement. She, too, could not believe that the leaders of the proletariat would be killed. The 11th of November, 1887, taught her differently. She realized that no mercy could be expected from the ruling class, that between the Tsarism of Russia and the plutocracy of America there was no difference save in name. Her whole being rebelled against the crime, and she vowed to herself a solemn vow to join the ranks of the revolutionary proletariat and to devote all her energy and strength to their emancipation from wage slavery. With the glowing enthusiasm so characteristic of her nature, she now began to familiarize herself with the literature of Socialism and Anarchism. She attended public meetings and became acquainted with socialistically and anarchistically inclined working-men. Johanna Greie, the well-known German lecturer, was the first Socialist speaker heard by Emma

Goldman. In New Haven, Conn., where she was employed in a corset factory, she met Anarchists actively participating in the movement. Here she read the *Freiheit,* edited by John Most. The Haymarket tragedy developed her inherent Anarchist tendencies; the reading of the *Freiheit* made her a conscious Anarchist. Subsequently she was to learn that the idea of Anarchism found its highest expression through the best intellects of America: theoretically by Josiah Warren, Stephen Pearl Andrews, Lysander Spooner; philosophically by Emerson, Thoreau, and Walt Whitman.

Made ill by the excessive strain of factory work, Emma Goldman returned to Rochester where she remained till August, 1889, at which time she removed to New York, the scene of the most important phase of her life. She was now twenty years old. Features pallid with suffering, eyes large and full of compassion, greet one in her pictured likeness of those days. Her hair is, as customary with Russian student girls, worn short, giving free play to the strong forehead.

It is the heroic epoch of militant Anarchism. By leaps and bounds the movement had grown in every country. In spite of the most severe governmental persecution new converts swell the ranks. The propaganda is almost exclusively of a secret character. The repressive measures of the government drive the disciples of the new philosophy to conspirative methods. Thousands of victims fall into the hands of the authorities and languish in prisons. But nothing can stem the rising tide of enthusiasm, of self-sacrifice and devotion to the Cause. The efforts of teachers like Peter Kropotkin, Louise Michel, Elisée Reclus, and others, inspire the devotees with ever greater energy. Disruption is imminent with the Socialists, who have sacrificed the idea of liberty and embraced the State and politics. The struggle is bitter, the factions irreconcilable. This struggle is not merely between Anarchists and Socialists.; it also finds its echo within the Anarchist groups. Theoretic differences and personal controversies lead to strife and acrimonious enmities. The anti-Socialist legislation of Germany and Austria had driven thousands of Socialists and Anarchists across the seas to seek refuge in America. John Most, having lost his seat in the Reichstag, finally had to flee his native land, and went to London. There, having advanced toward Anarchism, he entirely withdrew from the Social Democratic Party. Later, coming to America, he continued the publication of the *Freiheit* in New York, and developed great activity among the German workingmen.

When Emma Goldman arrived in New York in 1889, she experienced little difficulty in associating herself with active Anarchists. Anarchist meetings were an almost daily occurrence. The first lecturer she heard on the Anarchist platform was Dr. H. Solotaroff. Of great importance to her future development was her acquaintance with John Most, who exerted a tremendous influence over the younger elements. His impassioned eloquence, untiring energy, and the persecution he had endured for the Cause, all combined to enthuse the comrades. It was also at this period that she met Alexander Berkman, whose friendship played an important part throughout her life. Her talents as a speaker could not long remain in obscurity. The fire of enthusiasm swept her toward the public platform. Encouraged by her friends, she began to participate as a German and Yiddish speaker at Anarchist meetings. Soon followed a brief tour of agitation taking her as far as Cleveland. With the whole strength and earnestness of her soul she now threw herself into the propaganda of Anarchist ideas. The passionate period of her life had begun. Though constantly toiling in sweat-shops, the fiery young orator was at the same time very active as an agitator and participated in various labor struggles, notably in the great cloak-makers' strike, in 1889, led by Professor Garsyde and Joseph Barondess.

A year later Emma Goldman was a delegate to an Anarchist conference in New York. She was elected to the Executive Committee, but later withdrew because of differences of opinion regarding tactical matters. The ideas of the German-speaking Anarchists had at that time not yet become clarified. Some still believed in parliamentary methods, the great majority being adherents of strong centralism. These differences of opinion in regard to tactics led, in 1891, to a breach with John Most. Emma Goldman, Alexander Berkman, and other comrades joined the group *Autonomy*, in which Joseph Peukert, Otto Rinke, and Claus Timmermann played an active part.

The bitter controversies which followed this secession terminated only with the death of Most, in 1906.

A great source of inspiration to Emma Goldman proved the Russian revolutionists who were associated in the group *Znamya*. Goldenberg, Solotaroff, Zametkin, Miller, Cahan, the poet Edelstadt, Ivan von Schewitsch, husband of Helene von Racowitza and editor of the *Volkszeitung*, and numerous other Russian exiles, some of whom are still living, were members of the group. It was also at this time that Emma Goldman met Robert Reitzel, the German-American Heine, who exerted a great influence on her development. Through him she became acquainted with the best writers of modern literature, and the friendship thus begun lasted. till Reitzel's death, in 1898.

The labor movement of America had not been drowned in the Chicago massacre; the murder of the Anarchists had failed to bring peace to the profit-greedy capitalist. The struggle for the eight-hour day continued. In 1892 broke out the great strike in Pittsburg. The Homestead fight, the defeat of the Pinkertons, the appearance of the militia, the suppression of the strikers, and the complete triumph of the reaction are matters of comparatively recent history. Stirred to the very depths by the terrible events at the seat of war, Alexander Berkman resolved to sacrifice his life to the Cause and thus give an object lesson to the wage slaves of America of active Anarchist solidarity with labor. His attack upon Frick, the Gessler of Pittsburg, failed, and the twenty-two-year-old youth was doomed to a living death of twenty-two years in the penitentiary. The bourgeoisie, which for decades had exalted and eulogized tyrannicide, now was filled with terrible rage. The capitalist press organized a systematic campaign of calumny and misrepresentation against Anarchists. The police exerted every effort to involve Emma Goldman in the act of Alexander Berkman. The feared agitator was to be silenced by all means. It was only due to the circumstance of her presence in New York that she escaped the clutches of the law. It was a similar circumstance which, nine years later, during the McKinley incident, was instrumental in preserving her liberty. It is almost incredible with what amount of stupidity, baseness, and vileness the journalists of the period sought to overwhelm the Anarchist. One must peruse the newspaper files to realize the enormity of incrimination and slander. It would be difficult to portray the agony of soul Emma Goldman experienced in those days. The persecutions of the capitalist press were to be borne by an Anarchist with comparative equanimity; but the attacks from one's own ranks were far more painful and unbearable. The act of Berkman was severely criticized by Most and some of his followers among the German and Jewish Anarchists. Bitter accusations and recriminations at public meetings and private gatherings followed. Persecuted on all sides, both because she championed Berkman and his act, and on account of her revolutionary activity, Emma Goldman was harassed even to the extent of inability to secure shelter. Too proud to seek safety in the denial of her identity, she chose to pass the nights in the public parks rather than expose her friends to danger or vexation by her visits. The already bitter cup was filled to overflowing by the attempted suicide of a young comrade who had shared living quarters with Emma Goldman, Alexander Berkman, and a mutual artist friend.

Many changes have since taken place. Alexander Berkman has survived the Pennsylvania Inferno, and is back again in the ranks of the militant Anarchists, his spirit unbroken, his soul full of enthusiasm for the ideals of his youth. The artist comrade is now among the well-known illustrators of New York. The suicide candidate left America shortly after his unfortunate attempt to die, and was subsequently arrested and condemned to eight years of hard labor for smuggling Anarchist literature into Germany. He, too, has withstood the terrors of prison life, and has returned to the revolutionary movement, since earning the well deserved reputation of a talented writer in Germany.

To avoid indefinite camping in the parks Emma Goldman finally was forced to move into a house on Third Street, occupied exclusively by prostitutes. There, among the outcasts of our good Christian society, she could at least rent a bit of a room, and find rest and work at her sewing machine. The women of the street showed more refinement of feeling and sincere sympathy than the priests of the Church. But human endurance had been exhausted by overmuch suffering and privation. There was a complete physical breakdown, and the renowned agitator was removed to the "Bohemian Republic"— a large tenement house which derived its euphonious appellation from the fact that its occupants were mostly Bohemian Anarchists. Here Emma Goldman found friends ready to aid her. Justus Schwab, one of the finest representatives of the German revolutionary period of that time, and Dr. Solotaroff were indefatigable in the care of the patient. Here, too, she met Edward Brady, the new friendship subsequently ripening into close intimacy. Brady had been an active participant in the revolutionary movement of Austria and had, at the time of his acquaintance with Emma Goldman, lately been released from an Austrian prison after an incarceration of ten years.

Physicians diagnosed the illness as consumption, and the patient was advised to leave New York. She went to Rochester, in the hope that the home circle would help to restore her to health. Her parents had several years previously emigrated to America, settling in that city. Among the leading traits of the Jewish race is the strong attachment between the members of the family, and, especially, between parents and children. Though her conservative parents could not sympathize with the idealist aspirations of Emma Goldman and did not approve of her mode of life, they now received their sick daughter with open arms. The rest and care enjoyed in the parental home, and the cheering presence of the beloved sister Helene, proved so beneficial that within a short time she was sufficiently restored to resume her energetic activity.

There is no rest in the life of Emma Goldman. Ceaseless effort and continuous striving toward the conceived goal are the essentials of her nature. Too much precious time had already been wasted. It was imperative to resume her labors immediately. The country was in the throes of a crisis, and thousands of unemployed crowded the streets of the large industrial centers. Cold and hungry they tramped through the land in the vain search for work and bread. The Anarchists developed a strenuous propaganda among the unemployed and the strikers. A monster demonstration of striking cloakmakers and of the unemployed took place at Union Square, New York. Emma Goldman was one of the invited speakers. She delivered an impassioned speech, picturing in fiery words the misery of the wage-slave's life, and quoted the famous maxim of Cardinal Manning: "Necessity knows no law, and the starving man has a natural right to a share of his neighbor's bread." She concluded her exhortation with the words: "Ask for work. If they do not give you work, ask for bread. If they do not give you work or bread, then take bread."

The following day she left for Philadelphia, where she was to address a public meeting. The capitalist press again raised the alarm. If Socialists and Anarchists were to be permitted to continue agitating, there was imminent danger that the workingmen would soon learn to understand the manner in which they are robbed of the joy and happiness of life.

Such a possibility was to be prevented at all cost. The Chief of Police of New York, Byrnes, procured a court order for the arrest of Emma Goldman. She was detained by the Philadelphia authorities and incarcerated for several days in the Moyamensing prison, awaiting the extradition papers which Byrnes intrusted to Detective Jacobs. This man Jacobs (whom Emma Goldman again met several years later under very unpleasant circumstances) proposed to her, while she was returning a prisoner to New York, to betray the cause of labor. In the name of his superior, Chief Byrnes, he offered lucrative reward. How stupid men sometimes are! What poverty of psychologic observation to imagine the possibility of betrayal on the part of a young Russian idealist, who had willingly sacrificed all personal considerations to help in labor's emancipation.

In October, 1893, Emma Goldman was tried in the criminal courts of New York on the charge of inciting to riot. The "intelligent" jury ignored the testimony of the twelve witnesses for the defense in favor of the evidence given by one single man— Detective Jacobs. She was found guilty and sentenced to serve one year in the penitentiary at Blackwell's Island. Since the foundation of the Republic she was the first woman—Mrs. Surratt excepted—to be imprisoned for a political offense. Respectable society had long before stamped upon her the Scarlet Letter.

Emma Goldman passed her time in the penitentiary in the capacity of nurse in the prison hospital. Here she found opportunity to shed some rays of kindness into the dark lives of the unfortunates whose sisters of the street did not disdain two years previously to share with her the same house. She also found in prison opportunity to study English and its literature, and to familiarize herself with the great American writers. In Bret Harte, Mark Twain, Walt Whitman, Thoreau, and Emerson she found great treasures.

She left Blackwell's Island in the month of August, 1894, a woman of twenty-five, developed and matured, and intellectually transformed. Back into the arena, richer in experience, purified by suffering. She did not feel herself deserted and alone any more. Many hands were stretched out to welcome her. There were at the time numerous intellectual oases in New York. The saloon of Justus Schwab, at Number Fifty, First Street, was the center where gathered Anarchists, littérateurs, and bohemians. Among others she also met at this time a number of American Anarchists, and formed the friendship of Voltairine de Cleyre, Wm. C. Owen, Miss Van Etton, and Dyer D. Lum, former editor of the *Alarm* and executor of the last wishes of the Chicago martyrs. In John Swinton, the noble old fighter for liberty, she found one of her staunchest friends. Other intellectual centers there were: *Solidarity*, published by John Edelman; *Liberty*, by the Individualist Anarchist Benjamin R. Tucker; the *Rebel*, by Harry Kelly; *Der Sturmvogel*, a German Anarchist publication, edited by Claus Timmermann; *Der Arme Teufel*, whose presiding genius was the inimitable Robert Reitzel. Through Arthur Brisbane, now chief lieutenant of William Randolph

Hearst, she became acquainted with the writings of Fourier. Brisbane then was not yet submerged in the swamp of political corruption. He sent Emma Goldman an amiable letter to Blackwell's Island, together with the biography of his father, the enthusiastic American disciple of Fourier.

Emma Goldman became, upon her release from the penitentiary, a factor in the public life of New York. She was appreciated in radical ranks for her devotion, her idealism, and earnestness. Various persons sought her friendship, and some tried to persuade her to aid in the furtherance of their special side issues. Thus Rev. Parkhurst, during the Lexow investigation, did his utmost to induce her to join the Vigilance Committee in order to fight Tammany Hall. Maria Louise, the moving spirit of a social center, acted as Parkhurst's go-between. It is hardly necessary to mention what reply the latter received from Emma Goldman. Incidentally, Maria Louise subsequently became a Mahatma. During the free-silver campaign, ex-Burgess McLuckie, one of the most genuine personalities in the Homestead strike, visited New York in an endeavor to enthuse the local radicals for free silver. He also attempted to interest Emma Goldman, but with no greater success than Mahatma Maria Louise of Parkhurst-Lexow fame.

In 1894 the struggle of the Anarchists in France reached its highest expression. The white terror on the part of the Republican upstarts was answered by the red terror of our French comrades.

With feverish anxiety the Anarchists throughout the world followed this social struggle. Propaganda by deed found its reverberating echo in almost all countries. In order to better familiarize herself with conditions in the old world, Emma Goldman left for Europe, in the year 1895. After a lecture tour in England and Scotland, she went to Vienna where she entered the *Allgemeine Krankenhaus* to prepare herself as midwife and nurse, and where at the same time she studied social conditions. She also found opportunity to acquaint herself with the newest literature of Europe: Hauptmann, Nietzsche, Ibsen, Zola, Thomas Hardy, and other artist rebels were read with great enthusiasm.

In the autumn of 1896 she returned to New York by way of Zurich and Paris. The project of Alexander Berkman's liberation was on hand. The barbaric sentence of twenty-two years had roused tremendous indignation among the radical elements. It was known that the Pardon Board of Pennsylvania would look to Carnegie and Frick for advice in the case of Alexander Berkman. It was therefore suggested that these Sultans of Pennsylvania be approached—not with a view of obtaining their grace, but with the request that they do not attempt to influence the Board. Ernest Crosby offered to see Carnegie, on condition that Alexander Berkman repudiate his act. That, however, was absolutely out of the question. He would never be guilty of such forswearing of his own personality and self-respect. These efforts led to friendly relations between Emma Goldman and the circle of Ernest

Crosby, Bolton Hall, and Leonard Abbott. In the year 1897 she undertook her first great lecture tour, which extended as far as California. This tour popularized her name as the representative of the oppressed, her eloquence ringing from coast to coast. In California Emma Goldman became friendly with the members of the Isaak family, and learned to appreciate their efforts for the Cause. Under tremendous obstacles the Isaaks first published the *Firebrand* and, upon its suppression by the Postal Department, the *Free Society*. It was also during this tour that Emma Goldman met that grand old rebel of sexual freedom, Moses Harman.

During the Spanish-American war the spirit of chauvinism was at its highest tide. To check this dangerous situation, and at the same time collect funds for the revolutionary Cubans, Emma Goldman became affiliated with the Latin comrades, among others with Gori, Esteve, Palaviccini, Merlino, Petruccini, and Ferrara. In the year 1899 followed another protracted tour of agitation, terminating on the Pacific Coast. Repeated arrests and accusations, though without ultimate bad results, marked every propaganda tour.

In November of the same year the untiring agitator went on a second lecture tour to England and Scotland, closing her journey with the first International Anarchist Congress at Paris. It was at the time of the Boer war, and again jingoism was at its height, as two years previously it had celebrated its orgies during the Spanish-American war. Various meetings, both in England and Scotland, were disturbed and broken up by patriotic mobs. Emma Goldman found on this occasion the opportunity of again meeting various English comrades and interesting personalities like Tom Mann and the sisters Rossetti, the gifted daughters of Dante Gabriel Rossetti, then publishers of the Anarchist review, the *Torch.* One of her life-long hopes found here its fulfillment: she came in close and friendly touch with Peter Kropotkin, Enrico Malatesta, Nicholas Tchaikovsky, W. Tcherkessov, and Louise Michel. Old warriors in the cause of humanity, whose deeds have enthused thousands of followers throughout the world, and whose life and work have inspired other thousands with noble idealism and self-sacrifice. Old warriors they, yet ever young with the courage of earlier days, unbroken in spirit and filled with the firm hope of the final triumph of Anarchy.

The chasm in the revolutionary labor movement, which resulted from the disruption of the *Internationale,* could not be bridged any more. Two social philosophies were engaged in bitter combat. The International Congress in 1889, at Paris; in 1892, at Zurich, and in 1896, at London, produced irreconcilable differences. The majority of Social Democrats, forswearing their libertarian past and becoming politicians, succeeded in excluding the revolutionary and Anarchist delegates. The latter decided thenceforth to hold separate congresses. Their first congress was to take place in 1900, at Paris. The Socialist renegade Millerand, who had climbed into the Ministry of the Interior, here played a Judas rôle. The congress of the revolutionists was suppressed, and the delegates dispersed two days prior to the scheduled opening. But Millerand had no objections against the Social Democratic Congress, which was afterwards opened with all the trumpets of the advertiser's art.

However, the renegade did not accomplish his object. A number of delegates succeeded in holding a secret conference in the house of a comrade outside of Paris, where various points of theory and tactics were discussed. Emma Goldman took considerable part in these proceedings, and on that occasion came in contact with numerous representatives of the Anarchist movement of Europe.

Owing to the suppression of the congress, the delegates were in danger of being expelled from France. At this time also came the bad news from America regarding another unsuccessful attempt to liberate Alexander Berkman, proving a great shock to Emma Goldman. In November, 1900, she returned to America to devote herself to her profession of nurse, at the same time taking an active part in the American propaganda. Among other activities she organized monster meetings of protest against the terrible outrages of the Spanish government, perpetrated upon the political prisoners tortured in Montjuich.

In her vocation as nurse Emma Goldman enjoyed many opportunities of meeting the most unusual and peculiar characters. Few would have identified the "notorious Anarchist" in the small blonde woman, simply attired in the uniform of a nurse. Soon after her return from Europe she became acquainted with

a patient by the name of Mrs. Stander, a morphine
fiend, suffering excruciating agonies. She required
careful attention to enable her to supervise a very important business she conducted,—that of Mrs. Warren.
In Third Street, near Third Avenue, was situated her
private residence, and near it, connected by a separate
entrance, was her place of business. One evening,
the nurse, upon entering the room of her patient, suddenly came face to face with a male visitor, bull-
necked and of brutal appearance. The man was no
other than Mr. Jacobs, the detective who seven years
previously had brought Emma Goldman a prisoner
from Philadelphia and who had attempted to persuade her, on their way to New York, to betray the
cause of the workingmen. It would be difficult to
describe the expression of bewilderment on the coun-
tenance of the man as he so unexpectedly faced
Emma Goldman, the nurse of his mistress. The
brute was suddenly transformed into a gentleman,
exerting himself to excuse his shameful behavior on
the previous occasion. Jacobs was the "protector" of
Mrs. Stander, and go-between for the house and the
police. Several years later, as one of the detective
staff of District Attorney Jerome, he committed per-
jury, was convicted, and sent to Sing Sing for a year.
He is now probably employed by some private detective agency, a desirable pillar of respectable society.

In 1901 Peter Kropotkin was invited by the Lowell
Institute of Massachusetts to deliver a series of lectures on Russian literature. It was his second American tour, and naturally the comrades were anxious to
use his presence for the benefit of the movement.

Emma Goldman entered into correspondence with
Kropotkin and succeeded in securing his consent to
arrange for him a series of lectures. She also devoted her energies to organizing the tours of other
well known Anarchists, principally those of Charles
W. Mowbray and John Turner. Similarly she always
took part in all the activities of the movement, ever
ready to give her time, ability, and energy to the
Cause.

On the sixth of September, 1901, President Mc-
Kinley was shot by Leon Czolgosz at Buffalo. Immediately an unprecedented campaign of persecution
was set in motion against Emma Goldman as the best
known Anarchist in the country. Although there was
absolutely no foundation for the accusation, she,
together with other prominent Anarchists, was arrested in Chicago, kept in confinement for several weeks, and subjected to severest cross-examina-
tion. Never before in the history of the country had
such a terrible man-hunt taken place against a person in public life. But the efforts of police and press
to connect Emma Goldman with Czolgosz proved
futile. Yet the episode left her wounded to the heart.
The physical suffering, the humiliation and brutality at the hands of the police she could bear.
The depression of soul was far worse. She was overwhelmed by the realization of the stupidity, lack of
understanding, and vileness which characterized the
events of those terrible days. The attitude of mis-
understanding on the part of the majority of her
own comrades toward Czolgosz almost drove her to
desperation. Stirred to the very inmost of her soul,

she published an article on Czolgosz in which she tried to explain the deed in its social and individual aspects. As once before, after Berkman's act, she now also was unable to find quarters; like a veritable wild animal she was driven from place to place. This terrible persecution and, especially, the attitude of her comrades made it impossible for her to continue propaganda. The soreness of body and soul had first to heal. During 1901-1903 she did not resume the platform. As "Miss Smith" she lived a quiet life, practicing her profession and devoting her leisure to the study of literature and, particularly, to the modern drama, which she considers one of the greatest disseminators of radical ideas and enlightened feeling.

Yet one thing the persecution of Emma Goldman accomplished. Her name was brought before the public with greater frequency and emphasis than ever before, the malicious harassing of the much maligned agitator arousing strong sympathy in many circles. Persons in various walks of life began to get interested in her struggle and her ideas. A better understanding and appreciation were now beginning to manifest themselves.

The arrival in America of the English Anarchist, John Turner, induced Emma Goldman to leave her retirement. Again she threw herself into her public activities, organizing an energetic movement for the defense of Turner, whom the Immigration authorities condemned to deportation on account of the Anarchist exclusion law, passed after the death of McKinley.

When Paul Orleneff and Mme. Nazimova arrived in New York to acquaint the American public with Russian dramatic art, Emma Goldman became the manager of the undertaking. By much patience and perseverance she succeeded in raising the necessary funds to introduce the Russian artists to the theatergoers of New York and Chicago. Though financially not a success, the venture proved of great artistic value. As manager of the Russian theater Emma Goldman enjoyed some unique experiences. M. Orleneff could converse only in Russian, and "Miss Smith" was forced to act as his interpreter at various polite functions. Most of the aristocratic ladies of Fifth Avenue had not the least inkling that the amiable manager who so entertainingly discussed philosophy, drama, and literature at their five o'clock teas, was the "notorious" Emma Goldman. If the latter should some day write her autobiography, she will no doubt have many interesting anecdotes to relate in connection with these experiences.

The weekly Anarchist publication *Free Society*, issued by the Isaak family, was forced to suspend in consequence of the nation-wide fury that swept the country after the death of McKinley. To fill out the gap Emma Goldman, in co-operation with Max Baginski and other comrades, decided to publish a monthly magazine devoted to the furtherance of Anarchist ideas in life and literature. The first issue of *Mother Earth* appeared in the month of March, 1906, the initial expenses of the periodical partly covered by the proceeds of a theater benefit given by Orleneff, Mme. Nazimova, and their company, in favor of the Anarchist magazine. Under tremendous difficulties and obstacles the tireless propagandist has succeeded in continuing *Mother Earth* uninterruptedly since 1906—an achievement rarely equalled in the annals of radical publications.

In May, 1906, Alexander Berkman at last left the hell of Pennsylvania, where he had passed the best fourteen years of his life. No one had believed in the possibility of his survival. His liberation terminated a nightmare of fourteen years for Emma Goldman, and an important chapter of her career was thus concluded.

Nowhere had the birth of the Russian revolution aroused such vital and active response as among the Russians living in America. The heroes of the revolutionary movement in Russia, Tchaikovsky, Mme. Breshkovskaia, Gershuni, and others visited these shores to waken the sympathies of the American people toward the struggle for liberty, and to collect aid for its continuance and support. The success of these efforts was to a considerable extent due to the exertions, eloquence, and the talent for organization on the part of Emma Goldman. This opportunity enabled her to give valuable services to the struggle for liberty in her native land. It is not generally known that it is the Anarchists who are mainly instrumental in insuring the success, moral as well as financial, of most of the radical undertakings. The Anarchist is indifferent to acknowledged appreciation; the needs of the Cause absorb his whole interest, and to these he devotes his energy and abilities. Yet it may be mentioned that some otherwise decent folks, though at all times anxious for Anarchist support and co-operation, are ever willing to monopolize all the credit for the work done. During the last several decades it was chiefly the Anarchists who had organized all the great revolutionary efforts, and aided in every struggle for liberty. But for fear of shocking the respectable mob, who looks upon the Anarchists as the apostles of Satan, and because of their social position in bourgeois society, the would-be radicals ignore the activity of the Anarchists.

In 1907 Emma Goldman participated as delegate to the second Anarchist Congress, at Amsterdam. She was intensely active in all its proceedings and supported the organization of the Anarchist *Internationale*. Together with the other American delegate, Max Baginski, she submitted to the congress an exhaustive report of American conditions, closing with the following characteristic remarks:

"The charge that Anarchism is destructive, rather than constructive, and that, therefore, Anarchism is opposed to organization, is one of the many falsehoods spread by our opponents. They confound our present social institutions with organization; hence they fail to understand how we can oppose the former, and yet favor the latter. The fact, however, is that the two are not identical.

The State is commonly regarded as the highest form of organization. But is it in reality a true organization? Is it not rather an arbitrary institution, cunningly imposed upon the masses?

Industry, too, is called an organization; yet nothing is farther from the truth. Industry is the ceaseless piracy of the rich against the poor.

We are asked to believe that the Army is an organization, but a close investigation will show that it is nothing else than a cruel instrument of blind force.

The Public School! The colleges and other institutions of learning, are they not models of organization, offering the people fine opportunities for instruction? Far from it. The school, more than any other institution, is a veritable barrack, where the human mind is drilled and manipulated into submission to various social and moral spooks, and thus fitted to continue our system of exploitation and oppression.

Organization, as *we* understand it, however, is a different thing. It is based, primarily, on freedom. It is a natural and voluntary grouping of energies to secure results beneficial to humanity.

It is the harmony of organic growth which produces variety of color and form, the complete whole we admire in the flower. Analogously will the organized activity of free human beings, imbued with the spirit of solidarity, result in the perfection of social harmony, which we call Anarchism. In fact, Anarchism alone makes non-authoritarian organization of common interests possible, since it abolishes the existing antagonism between individuals and classes.

Under present conditions the antagonism of economic and social interests results in relentless war among the social units, and creates an insurmountable obstacle in the way of a co-operative commonwealth.

There is a mistaken notion that organization does not foster individual freedom; that, on the contrary, it means the decay of individuality. In reality, however, the true function of organization is to aid the development and growth of personality.

Just as the animal cells, by mutual co-operation, express their latent powers in formation of the complete organism, so does the individual, by co-operative effort with other individuals, attain his highest form of development.

An organization, in the true sense, cannot result from the combination of mere nonentities. It must be composed of self-conscious, intelligent individualities. Indeed, the total of the possibilities and activities of an organization is represented in the expression of individual energies.

It therefore logically follows that the greater the number of strong, self-conscious personalities in an organization, the less danger of stagnation, and the more intense its life element.

Anarchism asserts the possibility of an organization without discipline, fear, or punishment, and without the pressure of poverty: a new social organism which will make an end to the terrible struggle for the means of existence,—the savage struggle which undermines the finest qualities in man, and ever widens the social abyss. In short, Anarchism strives towards a social organization which will establish well-being for all.

The germ of such an organization can be found in that form of trades-unionism which has done away with centralization, bureaucracy, and discipline, and which favors independent and direct action on the part of its members."

The very considerable progress of Anarchist ideas in America can best be gauged by the remarkable success of the three extensive lecture tours of Emma Goldman since the Amsterdam Congress of 1907. Each tour extended over new territory, including localities where Anarchism had never before received a hearing. But the most gratifying aspect of her untiring efforts is the tremendous sale of Anarchist literature, whose propagandistic effect cannot be estimated. It was during one of these tours that a remarkable incident happened, strikingly demonstrating the inspiring potentialities of the Anarchist idea. In San Francisco, in 1908, Emma Goldman's lecture attracted a soldier of the United States Army, William Buwalda. For daring to attend an Anarchist meeting, the free Republic court-martialed Buwalda and imprisoned him for one year. Thanks to the regenerating power of the new philosophy, the government lost a soldier, but the cause of liberty gained a man.

A propagandist of Emma Goldman's importance is necessarily a sharp thorn to the reaction. She is looked upon as a danger to the continued existence of authoritarian usurpation. No wonder, then, that the enemy resorts to any and all means to make her impossible. A systematic attempt to suppress her activities was organized a year ago by the united police force of the country. But like all previous similar attempts, it failed in a most brilliant manner. Energetic protests on the part of the intellectual element of America succeeded in overthrowing the dastardly conspiracy against free speech. Another attempt to make Emma Goldman impossible was essayed by the Federal authorities at Washington. In order to deprive her of the rights of citizenship, the government revoked the citizenship papers of her husband, whom she had married at the youthful age of eighteen, and whose whereabouts, if he be alive, could not be determined for the last two decades. The great government of the glorious United States did not hesitate to stoop to the most despicable methods to accomplish that achievement. But as her citizenship had never proved of use to Emma Goldman, she can bear the loss with a light heart.

There are personalities who possess such a powerful individuality that by its very force they exert the most potent influence over the best representatives of their time. Michael Bakunin was such a personality. But for him, Richard Wagner had never written *Die Kunst und die Revolution*. Emma Goldman is a similar personality. She is a strong factor in the socio-political life of America. By virtue of her eloquence, energy, and brilliant mentality, she moulds the minds and hearts of thousands of her auditors.

Deep sympathy and compassion for suffering humanity, and an inexorable honesty toward herself, are the leading traits of Emma Goldman. No person, whether friend or foe, shall presume to control her goal or dictate her mode of life. She would perish rather than sacrifice her convictions, or the right of self-ownership of soul and body. Respectability could easily forgive the teaching of theoretic Anarchism; but Emma Goldman does not merely preach the new philosophy; she also persists in living it,—and that is the one supreme, unforgivable crime. Were she, like so many radicals, to consider her ideal as merely an intellectual ornament; were she to make concessions to existing society and compromise with old prejudices,—then even the most radical views could be pardoned in her. But that she takes her radicalism seriously; that it has permeated her blood and marrow to the extent where she not merely teaches but also practices her convictions—this shocks even the radical Mrs. Grundy. Emma Goldman lives her own life; she associates with publicans—hence the indignation of the Pharisees and Sadducees.

It is no mere coincidence that such divergent writers as Pietro Gori and William Marion Reedy find similar traits in their characterization of Emma Goldman. In a contribution to *La Questione Sociale*, Pietro Gori calls her a "moral power, a woman who, with the vision of a sibyl, prophesies the coming of a new kingdom for the oppressed; a woman who, with logic and deep earnestness, analyses the ills of society, and portrays, with artist touch, the coming dawn of humanity, founded on equality, brotherhood, and liberty."

William Reedy sees in Emma Goldman the "daughter of the dream, her gospel a vision which is the vision of every truly great-souled man and woman who has ever lived."

Cowards who fear the consequences of their deeds have coined the word of philosophic Anarchism. Emma Goldman is too sincere, too defiant, to seek safety behind such paltry pleas. She is an Anarchist, pure and simple. She represents the idea of Anarchism as framed by Josiah Warren, Proudhon, Bakunin, Kropotkin, Tolstoy. Yet she also understands the psychologic causes which induce a Caserio, a Vaillant, a Bresci, a Berkman, or a Czolgosz to commit deeds of violence. To the soldier in the social struggle it is a point of honor to come in conflict with the powers of darkness and tyranny, and Emma Goldman is proud to count among her best friends and comrades men and women who bear the wounds and scars received in battle.

In the words of Voltairine de Cleyre, characterizing Emma Goldman after the latter's imprisonment in 1893: The spirit that animates Emma Goldman is the only one which will emancipate the slave from his slavery, the tyrant from his tyranny—the spirit which is willing to dare and suffer.

HIPPOLYTE HAVEL.

New York, December, 1910.

PREFACE

SOME twenty-one years ago I heard the first great Anarchist speaker—the inimitable John Most. It seemed to me then, and for many years after, that the spoken word hurled forth among the masses with such wonderful eloquence, such enthusiasm and fire, could never be erased from the human mind and soul. How could any one of all the multitudes who flocked to Most's meetings escape his prophetic voice! Surely they had but to hear him to throw off their old beliefs, and see the truth and beauty of Anarchism!

My one great longing then was to be able to speak with the tongue of John Most,—that I, too, might thus reach the masses. Oh, for the naivety of Youth's enthusiasm! It is the time when the hardest thing seems but child's play. It is the only period in life worth while. Alas! This period is but of short duration. Like Spring, the *Sturm und Drang* period of the propagandist brings forth growth, frail and delicate, to be matured or killed according to its powers of resistance against a thousand vicissitudes.

My great faith in the wonder worker, the spoken word, is no more. I have realized its inadequacy to awaken thought, or even emotion. Gradually, and with no small struggle against this realization, I came to see that oral propaganda is at best but a means of shaking people from their lethargy: it leaves no lasting impression. The very fact that most people attend meetings only if aroused by newspaper sensations, or because they expect to be amused, is proof that they really have no inner urge to learn.

It is altogether different with the written mode of human expression. No one, unless intensely interested in progressive ideas, will bother with serious books. That leads me to another discovery made after many years of public activity. It is this: All claims of education notwithstanding, the pupil will accept only that which his mind craves. Already this truth is recognized by most modern educators in relation to the immature mind. I think it is equally true regarding the adult. Anarchists or revolutionists can no more be made than musicians. All that can be done is to plant the seeds of thought. Whether something vital will develop depends largely on the fertility of the human soil, though the quality of the intellectual seed must not be overlooked.

In meetings the audience is distracted by a thousand non-essentials. The speaker, though ever so eloquent, cannot escape the restlessness of the crowd, with the inevitable result that he will fail to strike root. In all probability he will not even do justice to himself.

The relation between the writer and the reader is more intimate. True, books are only what we want them to be; rather, what we read into them. That we

can do so demonstrates the importance of written
as against oral expression. It is this certainty which
has induced me to gather in one volume my ideas on
various topics of individual and social importance.
They represent the mental and soul struggles of
twenty-one years,—the conclusions derived after many
changes and inner revisions.

I am not sanguine enough to hope that my readers
will be as numerous as those who have heard me. But
I prefer to reach the few who really want to learn,
rather than the many who come to be amused.

As to the book, it must speak for itself. Ex-
planatory remarks do but detract from the ideas set
forth. However, I wish to forestall two objections
which will undoubtedly be raised. One is in reference
to the essay on *Anarchism;* the other, on *Minorities
versus Majorities.*

"Why do you not say how things will be operated
under Anarchism?" is a question I have had to meet
thousands of times. Because I believe that Anarchism
can not consistently impose an iron-clad program or
method on the future. The things every new generation has to fight, and which it can least overcome, are
the burdens of the past, which holds us all as in a net.
Anarchism, at least as I understand it, leaves posterity
free to develop its own particular systems, in harmony
with its needs. Our most vivid imagination can not
foresee the potentialities of a race set free from external restraints. How, then, can any one assume to
map out a line of conduct for those to come? We, who
pay dearly for every breath of pure, fresh air, must
guard against the tendency to fetter the future. If

we succeed in clearing the soil from the rubbish of the past and present, we will leave to posterity the greatest and safest heritage of all ages.

The most disheartening tendency common among readers is to tear out one sentence from a work, as a criterion of the writer's ideas or personality. Friedrich Nietzsche, for instance, is decried as a hater of the weak because he believed in the *Uebermensch*. It does not occur to the shallow interpreters of that giant mind that this vision of the *Uebermensch* also called for a state of society which will not give birth to a race of weaklings and slaves.

It is the same narrow attitude which sees in Max Stirner naught but the apostle of the theory "each for himself, the devil take the hind one." That Stirner's individualism contains the greatest social possibilities is utterly ignored. Yet, it is nevertheless true that if society is ever to become free, it will be so through liberated individuals, whose free efforts make society.

These examples bring me to the objection that will be raised to *Minorities versus Majorities*. No doubt, I shall be excommunicated as an enemy of the people, because I repudiate the mass as a creative factor. I shall prefer that rather than be guilty of the demagogic platitudes so commonly in vogue as a bait for the people. I realize the malady of the oppressed and disinherited masses only too well, but I refuse to prescribe the usual ridiculous palliatives which allow the patient neither to die nor to recover. One cannot be too extreme in dealing with social ills; besides, the extreme thing is generally the true thing. My lack of faith in the majority is dictated by my faith in the

potentialities of the individual. Only when the latter
becomes free to choose his associates for a common
purpose, can we hope for order and harmony out of
this world of chaos and inequality.

For the rest, my book must speak for itself.

Emma Goldman

ANARCHISM

WHAT IT REALLY STANDS FOR

ANARCHY.

Ever reviled, accursed, ne'er understood,
    Thou art the grisly terror of our age.
"Wreck of all order," cry the multitude,
    "Art thou, and war and murder's endless rage."
O, let them cry. To them that ne'er have striven
    The truth that lies behind a word to find,
To them the word's right meaning was not given.
    They shall continue blind among the blind.
But thou, O word, so clear, so strong, so pure,
    Thou sayest all which I for goal have taken.
I give thee to the future! Thine secure
    When each at least unto himself shall waken.
Comes it in sunshine? In the tempest's thrill?
    I cannot tell—but it the earth shall see!
I am an Anarchist! Wherefore I will
    Not rule, and also ruled I will not be!

                                JOHN HENRY MACKAY.

THE history of human growth and development is
at the same time the history of the terrible struggle
of every new idea heralding the approach of a brighter
dawn. In its tenacious hold on tradition, the Old

has never hesitated to make use of the foulest and cruelest means to stay the advent of the New, in whatever form or period the latter may have asserted itself. Nor need we retrace our steps into the distant past to realize the enormity of opposition, difficulties, and hardships placed in the path of every progressive idea. The rack, the thumbscrew, and the knout are still with us; so are the convict's garb and the social wrath, all conspiring against the spirit that is serenely marching on.

Anarchism could not hope to escape the fate of all other ideas of innovation. Indeed, as the most revolutionary and uncompromising innovator, Anarchism must needs meet with the combined ignorance and venom of the world it aims to reconstruct.

To deal even remotely with all that is being said and done against Anarchism would necessitate the writing of a whole volume. I shall therefore meet only two of the principal objections. In so doing, I shall attempt to elucidate what Anarchism really stands for.

The strange phenomenon of the opposition to Anarchism is that it brings to light the relation between so-called intelligence and ignorance. And yet this is not so very strange when we consider the relativity of all things. The ignorant mass has in its favor that it makes no pretense of knowledge or tolerance. Acting, as it always does, by mere impulse, its reasons are like those of a child. "Why?" "Because." Yet the opposition of the uneducated to Anarchism deserves the same consideration as that of the intelligent man.

What, then, are the objections? First, Anarchism is impractical, though a beautiful ideal. Second, Anarchism stands for violence and destruction, hence it must be repudiated as vile and dangerous. Both the intelligent man and the ignorant mass judge not from a thorough knowledge of the subject, but either from hearsay or false interpretation.

A practical scheme, says Oscar Wilde, is either one already in existence, or a scheme that could be carried out under the existing conditions; but it is exactly the existing conditions that one objects to, and any scheme that could accept these conditions is wrong and foolish. The true criterion of the practical, therefore, is not whether the latter can keep intact the wrong or foolish; rather is it whether the scheme has vitality enough to leave the stagnant waters of the old, and build, as well as sustain, new life. In the light of this conception, Anarchism is indeed practical. More than any other idea, it is helping to do away with the wrong and foolish; more than any other idea, it is building and sustaining new life.

The emotions of the ignorant man are continuously kept at a pitch by the most blood-curdling stories about Anarchism. Not a thing too outrageous to be employed against this philosophy and its exponents. Therefore Anarchism represents to the unthinking what the proverbial bad man does to the child,— a black monster bent on swallowing everything; in short, destruction and violence.

Destruction and violence! How is the ordinary man to know that the most violent element in society is ignorance; that its power of destruction is the very thing Anarchism is combating? Nor is he aware that Anarchism, whose roots, as it were, are part of nature's forces, destroys, not healthful tissue, but parasitic growths that feed on the life's essence of society. It is merely clearing the soil from weeds and sagebrush, that it may eventually bear healthy fruit.

Someone has said that it requires less mental effort to condemn than to think. The widespread mental indolence, so prevalent in society, proves this to be only too true. Rather than to go to the bottom of any given idea, to examine into its origin and meaning, most people will either condemn it altogether, or rely on some superficial or prejudicial definition of non-essentials.

Anarchism urges man to think, to investigate, to analyze every proposition; but that the brain capacity of the average reader be not taxed too much, I also shall begin with a definition, and then elaborate on the latter.

> ANARCHISM:—The philosophy of a new social order based on liberty unrestricted by man-made law; the theory that all forms of government rest on violence, and are therefore wrong and harmful, as well as unnecessary.

The new social order rests, of course, on the materialistic basis of life; but while all Anarchists agree that the main evil today is an economic one, they maintain that the solution of that evil can be brought about only through the consideration of *every phase* of life,—individual, as well as the collective; the internal, as well as the external phases.

A thorough perusal of the history of human development will disclose two elements in bitter conflict with each other; elements that are only now beginning to be understood, not as foreign to each other, but as closely related and truly harmonious, if only placed in proper environment: the individual and social instincts. The individual and society have waged a relentless and bloody battle for ages, each striving for supremacy, because each was blind to the value and importance of the other. The individual and social instincts,—the one a most potent factor for individual endeavor, for growth, aspiration, self-realization; the other an equally potent factor for mutual helpfulness and social well-being.

The explanation of the storm raging within the individual, and between him and his surroundings, is not far to seek. The primitive man, unable to understand his being, much less the unity of all life, felt himself absolutely dependent on blind, hidden forces ever ready to mock and taunt him. Out of that attitude grew the religious concepts of man as a mere speck of dust dependent on superior powers on high, who can only be appeased by complete surrender. All the early sagas rest on that idea, which continues to be the *Leitmotiv* of the biblical tales dealing with the relation of man to God, to the State, to society. Again and again the same motif, *man is nothing, the powers are everything.* Thus Jehovah would only endure man on condition of complete surrender. Man can have all the glories of the earth, but he must not become conscious of himself. The State, society, and moral laws all sing the same refrain: Man can have all the glories of the earth, but he must not become conscious of himself.

Anarchism is the only philosophy which brings to man the consciousness of himself; which maintains that God, the State, and society are non-existent, that their promises are null and void, since they can be fulfilled only through man's subordination. Anarchism is therefore the teacher of the unity of life; not merely in nature, but in man. There is no conflict between the individual and the social instincts, any more than there is between the heart and the lungs: the one the receptacle of a precious life essence, the other the repository of the element that keeps the essence pure and strong. The individual is the heart of society, conserving the essence of social life; society is the lungs which are distributing the element to keep the life essence—that is, the individual—pure and strong.

"The one thing of value in the world," says Emerson, "is the active soul; this every man contains within him. The soul active sees absolute truth and utters truth and creates." In other words, the individual instinct is the thing of value in the world. It is the true soul that sees and creates the truth alive, out of which is to come a still greater truth, the re-born social soul.

Anarchism is the great liberator of man from the phantoms that have held him captive; it is the arbiter and pacifier of the two forces for individual and social harmony. To accomplish that unity, Anarchism has declared war on the pernicious influences which have so far prevented the harmonious blending of individual and social instincts, the individual and society.

Religion, the dominion of the human mind; Property, the dominion of human needs; and Government, the dominion of human conduct, represent the stronghold of man's enslavement and all the horrors it entails. Religion! How it dominates man's mind, how it humiliates and degrades his soul. God is everything, man is nothing, says religion. But out of that nothing God has created a kingdom so despotic, so tyrannical, so cruel, so terribly exacting that naught but gloom and tears and blood have ruled the world since gods began. Anarchism rouses man to rebellion against this black monster. Break your mental fetters, says Anarchism to man, for not until you think and judge for yourself will you get rid of the dominion of darkness, the greatest obstacle to all progress.

Property, the dominion of man's needs, the denial of the right to satisfy his needs. Time was when property claimed a divine right, when it came to man with the same refrain, even as religion, "Sacrifice! Abnegate! Submit!" The spirit of Anarchism has lifted man from his prostrate position. He now stands erect, with his face toward the light. He has learned to see the insatiable, devouring, devastating nature of property, and he is preparing to strike the monster dead.

"Property is robbery," said the great French Anarchist Proudhon. Yes, but without risk and danger to the robber. Monopolizing the accumulated efforts of man, property has robbed him of his birth-

right, and has turned him loose a pauper and an outcast. Property has not even the time-worn excuse
that man does not create enough to satisfy all needs.
The A B C student of economics knows that the
productivity of labor within the last few decades far
exceeds normal demand. But what are normal
demands to an abnormal institution? The only
demand that property recognizes is its own glutton-
ous appetite for greater wealth, because wealth
means power; the power to subdue, to crush, to
exploit, the power to enslave, to outrage, to degrade.
America is particularly boastful of her great power,
her enormous national wealth. Poor America, of
what avail is all her wealth, if the individuals com-
prising the nation are wretchedly poor? If they live
in squalor, in filth, in crime, with hope and joy gone,
a homeless, soilless army of human prey.

It is generally conceded that unless the returns
of any business venture exceed the cost, bankruptcy
is inevitable. But those engaged in the business of
producing wealth have not yet learned even this
simple lesson. Every year the cost of production in
human life is growing larger (50,000 killed, 100,000
wounded in America last year); the returns to the
masses, who help to create wealth, are ever getting
smaller. Yet America continues to be blind to the
inevitable bankruptcy of our business of production.
Nor is this the only crime of the latter. Still more
fatal is the crime of turning the producer into a mere
particle of a machine, with less will and decision
than his master of steel and iron. Man is being
robbed not merely of the products of his labor, but

of the power of free initiative, of originality, and
the interest in, or desire for, the things he is making.
Real wealth consists in things of utility and
beauty, in things that help to create strong, beautiful
bodies and surroundings inspiring to live in. But
if man is doomed to wind cotton around a spool, or
dig coal, or build roads for thirty years of his life,
there can be no talk of wealth. What he gives to
the world is only gray and hideous things, reflecting
a dull and hideous existence,—too weak to live, too
cowardly to die. Strange to say, there are people
who extol this deadening method of centralized production as the proudest achievement of our age. They
fail utterly to realize that if we are to continue in
machine subserviency, our slavery is more complete
than was our bondage to the King. They do not
want to know that centralization is not only the death-
knell of liberty, but also of health and beauty, of
art and science, all these being impossible in a clock-
like, mechanical atmosphere.

Anarchism cannot but repudiate such a method
of production: its goal is the freest possible expression of all the latent powers of the individual.
Oscar Wilde defines a perfect personality as "one
who develops under perfect conditions, who is not
wounded, maimed, or in danger." A perfect personality, then, is only possible in a state of society where
man is free to choose the mode of work, the conditions of work, and the freedom to work. One to
whom the making of a table, the building of a house,
or the tilling of the soil, is what the painting is to
the artist and the discovery to the scientist,—the

result of inspiration, of intense longing, and deep interest in work as a creative force. That being the ideal of Anarchism, its economic arrangements must consist of voluntary productive and distributive asso ciations, gradually developing into free communism, as the best means of producing with the least waste of human energy. Anarchism, however, also recognizes the right of the individual, or numbers of individuals, to arrange at all times for other forms of work, in harmony with their tastes and desires.

Such free display of human energy being possible only under complete individual and social freedom, Anarchism directs its forces against the third and greatest foe of all social equality; namely, the State, organized authority, or statutory law,—the dominion of human conduct.

Just as religion has fettered the human mind, and as property, or the monopoly of things, has subdued and stifled man's needs, so has the State enslaved his spirit, dictating every phase of conduct. "All government in essence," says Emerson, "is tyranny." It matters not whether it is government by divine right or majority rule. In every instance its aim is the absolute subordination of the individual.

Referring to the American government, the greatest American Anarchist, David Thoreau, said: "Government, what is it but a tradition, though a recent one, endeavoring to transmit itself unimpaired to posterity, but each instance losing its integrity; it has not the vitality and force of a single living man. Law never made man a whit more just; and by means of their respect for it, even the well disposed are daily made agents of injustice."

Indeed, the keynote of government is injustice. With the arrogance and self-sufficiency of the King who could do no wrong, governments ordain, judge, condemn, and punish the most insignificant offenses, while maintaining themselves by the greatest of all offenses, the annihilation of individual liberty. Thus Ouida is right when she maintains that "the State only aims at instilling those qualities in its public by which its demands are obeyed, and its exchequer is filled. Its highest attainment is the reduction of mankind to clockwork. In its atmosphere all those finer and more delicate liberties, which require treatment and spacious expansion, inevitably dry up and perish. The State requires a taxpaying machine in which there is no hitch, an exchequer in which there is never a deficit, and a public, monotonous, obedient, colorless, spiritless, moving humbly like a flock of sheep along a straight high road between two walls."

Yet even a flock of sheep would resist the chicanery of the State, if it were not for the corruptive, tyrannical, and oppressive methods it employs to serve its purposes. Therefore Bakunin repudiates the State as synonymous with the surrender of the liberty of the individual or small minorities,—the destruction of social relationship, the curtailment, or complete denial even, of life itself, for its own aggrandizement. The State is the altar of political freedom and, like the religious altar, it is maintained for the purpose of human sacrifice.

In fact, there is hardly a modern thinker who

does not agree that government, organized authority, or the State, is necessary *only* to maintain or protect property and monopoly. It has proven efficient in that function only.

Even George Bernard Shaw, who hopes for the miraculous from the State under Fabianism, nevertheless admits that "it is at present a huge machine for robbing and slave-driving of the poor by brute force." This being the case, it is hard to see why the clever prefacer wishes to uphold the State after poverty shall have ceased to exist.

Unfortunately there are still a number of people who continue in the fatal belief that government rests on natural laws, that it maintains social order and harmony, that it diminishes crime, and that it prevents the lazy man from fleecing his fellows. I shall therefore examine these contentions.

A natural law is that factor in man which asserts itself freely and spontaneously without any external force, in harmony with the requirements of nature. For instance, the demand for nutrition, for sex gratification, for light, air, and exercise, is a natural law. But its expression needs not the machinery of government, needs not the club, the gun, the handcuff, or the prison. To obey such laws, if we may call it obedience, requires only spontaneity and free opportunity. That governments do not maintain themselves through such harmonious factors is proven by the terrible array of violence, force, and coercion all governments use in order to live. Thus Blackstone is right when he says, "Human laws are invalid, because they are contrary to the laws of nature."

Unless it be the order of Warsaw after the slaughter of thousands of people, it is difficult to ascribe to governments any capacity for order or social harmony. Order derived through submission and maintained by terror is not much of a safe guaranty; yet that is the only "order" that governments have ever maintained. True social harmony grows naturally out of solidarity of interests. In a society where those who always work never have anything, while those who never work enjoy everything, solidarity of interests is non-existent; hence social harmony is but a myth. The only way organized authority meets this grave situation is by extending still greater privileges to those who have already monopolized the earth, and by still further enslaving the disinherited masses. Thus the entire arsenal of government—laws, police, soldiers, the courts, legislatures, prisons,—is strenuously engaged in "harmonizing" the most antagonistic elements in society.

The most absurd apology for authority and law is that they serve to diminish crime. Aside from the fact that the State is itself the greatest criminal, breaking every written and natural law, stealing in the form of taxes, killing in the form of war and capital punishment, it has come to an absolute standstill in coping with crime. It has failed utterly to destroy or even minimize the horrible scourge of its own creation.

Crime is naught but misdirected energy. So long as every institution of today, economic, political, social, and moral, conspires to misdirect human energy into wrong channels; so long as most people are out of place doing the things they hate to do, living a life they loathe to live, crime will be inevitable, and all the laws on the statutes can only increase, but never do away with, crime. What does society, as it exists today, know of the process of despair, the poverty, the horrors, the fearful struggle the human soul must pass on its way to crime and degradation. Who that knows this terrible process can fail to see the truth in these words of Peter Kropotkin:

"Those who will hold the balance between the benefits thus attributed to law and punishment and the degrading effect of the latter on humanity; those who will estimate the torrent of depravity poured abroad in human society by the informer, favored by the Judge even, and paid for in clinking cash by governments, under the pretext of aiding to unmask crime; those who will go within prison walls and there see what human beings become when deprived of liberty, when subjected to the care of brutal keepers, to coarse, cruel words, to a thousand stinging, piercing humiliations, will agree with us that the entire apparatus of prison and punishment is an abomination which ought to be brought to an end."

The deterrent influence of law on the lazy man is too absurd to merit consideration. If society were only relieved of the waste and expense of keeping a lazy class, and the equally great expense of the paraphernalia of protection this lazy class requires, the social tables would contain an abundance for all, including even the occasional lazy individual. Besides, it is well to consider that laziness results either from special privileges, or physical and mental abnormalities. Our present insane system of production fosters both, and the most astounding phenomenon is that people should want to work at all now. Anarchism aims to strip labor of its deadening, dulling aspect, of its gloom and compulsion. It aims to make work an instrument of joy, of strength, of color, of real harmony, so that the poorest sort of a man should find in work both recreation and hope.

To achieve such an arrangement of life, government, with its unjust, arbitrary, repressive measures, must be done away with. At best it has but imposed one single mode of life upon all, without regard to individual and social variations and needs. In destroying government and statutory laws, Anarchism proposes to rescue the self-respect and independence of the individual from all restraint and invasion by authority. Only in freedom can man grow to his full stature. Only in freedom will he learn to think and move, and give the very best in him. Only in freedom will he realize the true force of the social bonds which knit men together, and which are the true foundation of a normal social life.

But what about human nature? Can it be changed? And if not, will it endure under Anarchism?

Poor human nature, what horrible crimes have been committed in thy name! Every fool, from king to policeman, from the flatheaded parson to the visionless dabbler in science, presumes to speak authoritatively of human nature. The greater the mental charlatan, the more definite his insistence on the wickedness and weaknesses of human nature. Yet, how can any one speak of it to-day, with every soul in a prison, with every heart fettered, wounded, and maimed?

John Burroughs has stated that experimental study of animals in captivity is absolutely useless. Their character, their habits, their appetites undergo a complete transformation when torn from their soil in field and forest. With human nature caged in a narrow space, whipped daily into submission, how can we speak of its potentialities?

Freedom, expansion, opportunity, and, above all, peace and repose, alone can teach us the real dominant factors of human nature and all its wonderful possibilities.

Anarchism, then, really stands for the liberation of the human mind from the dominion of religion; the liberation of the human body from the dominion of property; liberation from the shackles and restraint of government. Anarchism stands for a social order based on the free grouping of individuals for the purpose of producing real social wealth; an order that will guarantee to every human being free access to the earth and full enjoyment of the necessities of life, according to individual desires, tastes, and inclinations.

This is not a wild fancy or an aberration of the mind. It is the conclusion arrived at by hosts of intellectual men and women the world over; a conclusion resulting from the close and studious observation of the tendencies of modern society: individual liberty and economic equality, the twin forces for the birth of what is fine and true in man.

As to methods. Anarchism is not, as some may suppose, a theory of the future to be realized through divine inspiration. It is a living force in the affairs of our life, constantly creating new conditions. The methods of Anarchism therefore do not comprise an iron-clad program to be carried out under all circumstances. Methods must grow out of the economic needs of each place and clime, and of the intellectual and temperamental requirements of the individual. The serene, calm character of a Tolstoy will wish different methods for social reconstruction than the intense, overflowing personality of a Michael Bakunin or a Peter Kropotkin. Equally so it must be apparent that the economic and political needs of Russia will dictate more drastic measures than would England or America. Anarchism does not stand for military drill and uniformity; it does, however, stand for the spirit of revolt, in whatever form, against everything that hinders human growth. All Anarchists agree in that, as they also agree in their opposition to the political machinery as a means of bringing about the great social change.

"All voting," says Thoreau, "is a sort of gaming, like checkers, or backgammon, a playing with right and wrong; its obligation never exceeds that of expediency. Even voting for the right thing is doing nothing for it. A wise man will not leave the right to the mercy of chance, nor wish it to prevail through the power of the majority." A close examination of the machinery of politics and its achievements will bear out the logic of Thoreau.

What does the history of parliamentarism show? Nothing but failure and defeat, not even a single reform to ameliorate the economic and social stress of the people. Laws have been passed and enactments made for the improvement and protection of labor. Thus it was proven only last year that Illinois, with the most rigid laws for mine protection, had the greatest mine disasters. In States where child labor laws prevail, child exploitation is at its highest, and though with us the workers enjoy full political opportunities, capitalism has reached the most brazen zenith.

Even were the workers able to have their own representatives, for which our good Socialist politicians are clamoring, what chances are there for their honesty and good faith? One has but to bear in mind the process of politics to realize that its path of good intentions is full of pitfalls: wirepulling, intriguing, flattering, lying, cheating; in fact, chicanery of every description, whereby the political aspirant can achieve success. Added to that is a complete demoralization of character and conviction, until nothing is left that would make one hope for anything from such a human derelict. Time and time again the people were foolish enough to trust, believe, and support with their last farthing aspiring politicians, only to find themselves betrayed and cheated.

It may be claimed that men of integrity would not become corrupt in the political grinding mill. Perhaps not; but such men would be absolutely helpless to exert the slightest influence in behalf of labor, as indeed has been shown in numerous instances. The State is the economic master of its servants. Good men, if such there be, would either remain true to their political faith and lose their economic support, or they would cling to their economic master and be utterly unable to do the slightest good. The political arena leaves one no alternative, one must either be a dunce or a rogue.

The political superstition is still holding sway over the hearts and minds of the masses, but the true lovers of liberty will have no more to do with it. Instead, they believe with Stirner that man has as much liberty as he is willing to take. Anarchism therefore stands for direct action, the open defiance of, and resistance to, all laws and restrictions, economic, social, and moral. But defiance and resistance are illegal. Therein lies the salvation of man. Everything illegal necessitates integrity, self-reliance, and courage. In short, it calls for free, independent spirits, for "men who are men, and who have a bone in their backs which you cannot pass your hand through."

Universal suffrage itself owes its existence to direct action. If not for the spirit of rebellion, of the defiance on the part of the American revolutionary fathers, their posterity would still wear the King's coat. If not for the direct action of a John

Brown and his comrades, America would still trade in the flesh of the black man. True, the trade in white flesh is still going on; but that, too, will have to be abolished by direct action. Trade-unionism, the economic arena of the modern gladiator, owes its existence to direct action. It is but recently that law and government have attempted to crush the trade-union movement, and condemned the exponents of man's right to organize to prison as conspirators. Had they sought to assert their cause through begging, pleading, and compromise, trade-unionism would today be a negligible quantity. In France, in Spain, in Italy, in Russia, nay even in England (witness the growing rebellion of English labor unions), direct, revolutionary, economic action has become so strong a force in the battle for industrial liberty as to make the world realize the tremendous importance of labor's power. The General Strike, the supreme expression of the economic consciousness of the workers, was ridiculed in America but a short time ago. Today every great strike, in order to win, must realize the importance of the solidaric general protest.

Direct action, having proven effective along economic lines, is equally potent in the environment of the individual. There a hundred forces encroach upon his being, and only persistent resistance to them will finally set him free. Direct action against the authority in the shop, direct action against the authority of the law, direct action against the invasive, meddlesome authority of our moral code, is the logical, consistent method of Anarchism.

Will it not lead to a revolution? Indeed, it will. No real social change has ever come about without a revolution. People are either not familiar with their history, or they have not yet learned that revolution is but thought carried into action.

Anarchism, the great leaven of thought, is today permeating every phase of human endeavor. Science, art, literature, the drama, the effort for economic betterment, in fact every individual and social opposition to the existing disorder of things, is illumined by the spiritual light of Anarchism. It is the philosophy of the sovereignty of the individual. It is the theory of social harmony. It is the great, surging, living truth that is reconstructing the world, and that will usher in the Dawn.

MINORITIES VERSUS MAJORITIES

If I WERE to give a summary of the tendency of our times, I would say, Quantity. The multitude, the mass spirit, dominates everywhere, destroying quality. Our entire life—production, politics, and education—rests on quantity, on numbers. The worker who once took pride in the thoroughness and quality of his work, has been replaced by brainless, incompetent automatons, who turn out enormous quantities of things, valueless to themselves, and generally injurious to the rest of mankind. Thus quantity, instead of adding to life's comforts and peace, has merely increased man's burden.

In politics, naught but quantity counts. In proportion to its increase, however, principles, ideals, justice, and uprightness are completely swamped by the array of numbers. In the struggle for supremacy the various political parties outdo each other in trickery, deceit, cunning, and shady machinations, confident that the one who succeeds is sure to be hailed by the majority as the victor. That is the only god,—Success. As to what expense, what terrible cost to character, is of no moment. We have not far to go in search of proof to verify this sad fact.

Never before did the corruption, the complete rottenness of our government stand so thoroughly exposed; never before were the American people brought face to face with the Judas nature of that political body, which has claimed for years to be absolutely beyond reproach, as the mainstay of our institutions, the true protector of the rights and liberties of the people.

Yet when the crimes of that party became so brazen that even the blind could see them, it needed but to muster up its minions, and its supremacy was assured. Thus the very victims, duped, betrayed, outraged a hundred times, decided, not against, but in favor of the victor. Bewildered, the few asked how could the majority betray the traditions of American liberty? Where was its judgment, its reasoning capacity? That is just it, the majority cannot reason; it has no judgment. Lacking utterly in originality and moral courage, the majority has always placed its destiny in the hands of others. Incapable of standing responsibilities, it has followed its leaders even unto destruction. Dr. Stockman was right: "The most dangerous enemies of truth and justice in our midst are the compact majorities, the damned compact majority." Without ambition or initiative, the compact mass hates nothing so much as innovation. It has always opposed, condemned, and hounded the innovator, the pioneer of a new truth.

The oft repeated slogan of our time is, among all politicians, the Socialists included, that ours is an era of individualism, of the minority. Only those who do not probe beneath the surface might be led

to entertain this view. Have not the few accumulated the wealth of the world? Are they not the
masters, the absolute kings of the situation? Their
success, however, is due not to individualism, but to
the inertia, the cravenness, the utter submission of
the mass. The latter wants but to be dominated, to
be led, to be coerced. As to individualism, at no
time in human history did it have less chance of
expression, less opportunity to assert itself in a
normal, healthy manner.

The individual educator imbued with honesty of
purpose, the artist or writer of original ideas, the
independent scientist or explorer, the non-compromising pioneers of social changes are daily pushed to the
wall by men whose learning and creative ability have
become decrepit with age.

Educators of Ferrer's type are nowhere tolerated,
while the dietitians of predigested food, à la Pro-
fessors Eliot and Butler, are the successful perpetu-
ators of an age of nonentities, of automatons. In the
literary and dramatic world, the Humphrey Wards
and Clyde Fitches are the idols of the mass, while
but few know or appreciate the beauty and genius of
an Emerson, Thoreau, Whitman; an Ibsen, a Hauptmann, a Butler Yeats, or a Stephen Phillips. They
are like solitary stars, far beyond the horizon of
the multitude.

Publishers, theatrical managers, and critics ask not
for the quality inherent in creative art, but will it meet
with a good sale, will it suit the palate of the people?
Alas, this palate is like a dumping ground; it relishes
anything that needs no mental mastication. As a re-

sult, the mediocre, the ordinary, the commonplace represents the chief literary output.

Need I say that in art we are confronted with the same sad facts? One has but to inspect our parks and thoroughfares to realize the hideousness and vulgarity of the art manufacture. Certainly, none but a majority taste would tolerate such an outrage on art. False in conception and barbarous in execution, the statuary that infests American cities has as much relation to true art, as a totem to a Michael Angelo. Yet that is the only art that succeeds. The true artistic genius, who will not cater to accepted notions, who exercises originality, and strives to be true to life, leads an obscure and wretched existence. His work may some day become the fad of the mob, but not until his heart's blood had been exhausted; not until the pathfinder has ceased to be, and a throng of an idealless and visionless mob has done to death the heritage of the master.

It is said that the artist of today cannot create because Prometheuslike he is bound to the rock of economic necessity. This, however, is true of art in all ages. Michael Angelo was dependent on his patron saint, no less than the sculptor or painter of today, except that the art connoisseurs of those days were far away from the madding crowd. They felt honored to be permitted to worship at the shrine of the master.

The art protector of our time knows but one criterion, one value,—the dollar. He is not concerned about the quality of any great work, but in the quantity of dollars his purchase implies. Thus the finan-

cier in Mirbeau's *Les Affaires sont les Affaires* points
to some blurred arrangement in colors, saying: "See
I ow great it is; it cost 50,000 francs." Just like our
own parvenus. The fabulous figures paid for their
great art discoveries must make up for the poverty
of their taste.

The most unpardonable sin in society is independence of thought. That this should be so terribly
apparent in a country whose symbol is democracy, is
very significant of the tremendous power of the
majority.

Wendell Phillips said fifty years ago: "In our
country of absolute democratic equality, public opinion is not only omnipotent, it is omnipresent. There
is no refuge from its tyranny, there is no hiding from
its reach, and the result is that if you take the old
Greek lantern and go about to seek among a hundred, you will not find a single American who has
not, or who does not fancy at least he has, something to gain or lose in his ambition, his social life,
or business, from the good opinion and the votes of
those around him. And the consequence is that instead of being a mass of individuals, each one fear-
lessly blurting out his own conviction, as a nation
compared to other nations we are a mass of cowards.
More than any other people we are afraid of each
other." Evidently we have not advanced very far
from the condition that confronted Wendell Phillips.

Today, as then, public opinion is the omnipresent
tyrant; today, as then, the majority represents a mass
of cowards, willing to accept him who mirrors its
own soul and mind poverty. That accounts for the

unprecedented rise of a man like Roosevelt. He em
bodies the very worst element of mob psychology.
A politician, he knows that the majority cares little
for ideals or integrity. What it craves is display.
It matters not whether that be a dog show, a prize
fight, the lynching of a "nigger," the rounding up
of some petty offender, the marriage exposition of
an heiress, or the acrobatic stunts of an ex-president.
The more hideous the mental contortions, the greater
the delight and bravos of the mass. Thus, poor in
ideals and vulgar of soul, Roosevelt continues to be
the man of the hour.

On the other hand, men towering high above such
political pygmies, men of refinement, of culture, of
ability, are jeered into silence as mollycoddles. It is
absurd to claim that ours is the era of individualism.
Ours is merely a more poignant repetition of the
phenomenon of all history: every effort for progress,
for enlightenment, for science, for religious, political,
and economic liberty, emanates from the minority,
and not from the mass. Today, as ever, the few are
misunderstood, hounded, imprisoned, tortured, and
killed.

The principle of brotherhood expounded by the
agitator of Nazareth preserved the germ of life, of
truth and justice, so long as it was the beacon light
of the few. The moment the majority seized upon
it, that great principle became a shibboleth and harbinger of blood and fire, spreading suffering and
disaster. The attack on the omnipotence of Rome,
led by the colossal figures of Huss, Calvin, and
Luther, was like a sunrise amid the darkness of the

night. But so soon as Luther and Calvin turned politicians and began catering to the small potentates, the nobility, and the mob spirit, they jeopardized the great possibilities of the Reformation. They won success and the majority, but that majority proved no less cruel and bloodthirsty in the persecution of thought and reason than was the Catholic monster. Woe to the heretics, to the minority, who would not bow to its dicta. After infinite zeal, endurance, and sacrifice, the human mind is at last free from the religious phantom; the minority has gone on in pursuit of new conquests, and the majority is lagging behind, handicapped by truth grown false with age.

Politically the human race would still be in the most absolute slavery, were it not for the John Balls, the Wat Tylers, the Tells, the innumerable individual giants who fought inch by inch against the power of kings and tyrants. But for individual pioneers the world would have never been shaken to its very roots by that tremendous wave, the French Revolution. Great events are usually preceded by apparently small things. Thus the eloquence and fire of Camille Desmoulins was like the trumpet before Jericho, razing to the ground that emblem of torture, of abuse, of horror, the Bastille.

Always, at every period, the few were the banner bearers of a great idea, of liberating effort. Not so the mass, the leaden weight of which does not let it move. The truth of this is borne out in Russia with greater force than elsewhere. Thousands of lives have already been consumed by that bloody régime, yet the monster on the throne is not appeased.

How is such a thing possible when ideas, culture, literature, when the deepest and finest emotions groan under the iron yoke? The majority, that compact, immobile, drowsy mass, the Russian peasant, after a century of struggle, of sacrifice, of untold misery, still believes that the rope which strangles "the man with the white hands"* brings luck.

In the American struggle for liberty, the majority was no less of a stumbling block. Until this very day the ideas of Jefferson, of Patrick Henry, of Thomas Paine, are denied and sold by their posterity. The mass wants none of them. The greatness and courage worshipped in Lincoln have been forgotten in the men who created the background for the panorama of that time. The true patron saints of the black men were represented in that handful of fighters in Boston, Lloyd Garrison, Wendell Phillips, Thoreau, Margaret Fuller, and Theodore Parker, whose great courage and sturdiness culminated in that somber giant John Brown. Their untiring zeal, their eloquence and perseverance undermined the stronghold of the Southern lords. Lincoln and his minions followed only when abolition had become a practical issue, recognized as such by all.

About fifty years ago, a meteorlike idea made its appearance on the social horizon of the world, an idea so far-reaching, so revolutionary, so all-embracing as to spread terror in the hearts of tyrants everywhere. On the other hand, that idea was a harbinger of joy, of cheer, of hope to the millions. The pioneers

---

* The intellectuals.

knew the difficulties in their way, they knew the
opposition, the persecution, the hardships that would
meet them, but proud and unafraid they started on
their march onward, ever onward. Now that idea
has become a popular slogan. Almost everyone is
a Socialist today: the rich man, as well as his poor
victim; the upholders of law and authority, as well
as their unfortunate culprits; the freethinker, as well
as the perpetuator of religious falsehoods; the fashionable lady, as well as the shirtwaist girl. Why
not? Now that the truth of fifty years ago has become a lie, now that it has been clipped of all its
youthful imagination, and been robbed of its vigor,
its strength, its revolutionary ideal—why not? Now
that it is no longer a beautiful vision, but a "practical,
workable scheme," resting on the will of the majority,
why not? Political cunning ever sings the praise of
the mass: the poor majority, the outraged, the abused,
the giant majority, if only it would follow us.

Who has not heard this litany before? Who does
not know this never-varying refrain of all politicians?
That the mass bleeds, that it is being robbed and
exploited, I know as well as our vote-baiters. But
I insist that not the handful of parasites, but the
mass itself is responsible for this horrible state of
affairs. It clings to its masters, loves the whip, and
is the first to cry Crucify! the moment a protesting
voice is raised against the sacredness of capitalistic
authority or any other decayed institution. Yet how
long would authority and private property exist, if
not for the willingness of the mass to become soldiers,
policemen, jailers, and hangmen. The Socialist dema-

gogues know that as well as I, but they maintain the myth of the virtues of the majority, because their very scheme of life means the perpetuation of power. And how could the latter be acquired without numbers? Yes, authority, coercion, and dependence rest on the mass, but never freedom or the free unfoldment of the individual, never the birth of a free society.

Not because I do not feel with the oppressed, the disinherited of the earth; not because I do not know the shame, the horror, the indignity of the lives the people lead, do I repudiate the majority as a creative force for good. Oh, no, no! But because I know so well that as a compact mass it has never stood for justice or equality. It has suppressed the human voice, subdued the human spirit, chained the human body. As a mass its aim has always been to make life uniform, gray, and monotonous as the desert. As a mass it will always be the annihilator of individuality, of free initiative, of originality. I therefore believe with Emerson that "the masses are crude, lame, pernicious in their demands and influence, and need not to be flattered, but to be schooled. I wish not to concede anything to them, but to drill, divide, and break them up, and draw individuals out of them. Masses! The calamity are the masses. I do not wish any mass at all, but honest men only, lovely, sweet, accomplished women only."

In other words, the living, vital truth of social and economic well-being will become a reality only through the zeal, courage, the non-compromising determination of intelligent minorities, and not through the mass.

THE PSYCHOLOGY OF POLITICAL VIOLENCE

To ANALYZE the psychology of political violence is not only extremely difficult, but also very dangerous. If such acts are treated with understanding, one is immediately accused of eulogizing them. If, on the other hand, human sympathy is expressed with the *Attentäter*,* one risks being considered a possible accomplice. Yet it is only intelligence and sympathy that can bring us closer to the source of human suffering, and teach us the ultimate way out of it.

The primitive man, ignorant of natural forces, dreaded their approach, hiding from the perils they threatened. As man learned to understand Nature's phenomena, he realized that though these may destroy life and cause great loss, they also bring relief. To the earnest student it must be apparent that the accumulated forces in our social and economic life, culminating in a political act of violence, are similar to the terrors of the atmosphere, manifested in storm and lightning.

To thoroughly appreciate the truth of this view, one must feel intensely the indignity of our social

---

* A revolutionist committing an act of political violence.

wrongs; one's very being must throb with the pain, the sorrow, the despair millions of people are daily made to endure. Indeed, unless we have become a part of humanity, we cannot even faintly understand the just indignation that accumulates in a human soul, the burning, surging passion that makes the storm inevitable.

The ignorant mass looks upon the man who makes a violent protest against our social and economic iniquities as upon a wild beast, a cruel, heartless monster, whose joy it is to destroy life and bathe in blood; or at best, as upon an irresponsible lunatic. Yet nothing is further from the truth. As a matter of fact, those who have studied the character and personality of these men, or who have come in close contact with them, are agreed that it is their super-sensitiveness to the wrong and injustice surrounding them which compels them to pay the toll of our social crimes. The most noted writers and poets, discussing the psychology of political offenders, have paid them the highest tribute. Could anyone assume that these men had advised violence, or even approved of the acts? Certainly not. Theirs was the attitude of the social student, of the man who knows that beyond every violent act there is a vital cause.

Björnstjerne Björnson, in the second part of *Beyond Human Power,* emphasizes the fact that it is among the Anarchists that we must look for the modern martyrs who pay for their faith with their blood, and who welcome death with a smile, because they believe, as truly as Christ did, that their martyr-dom will redeem humanity.

François Coppé, the French novelist, thus expresses himself regarding the psychology of the *Attentäter:*
"The reading of the details of Vaillant's execution left me in a thoughtful mood. I imagined him expanding his chest under the ropes, marching with firm step, stiffening his will, concentrating all his energy, and, with eyes fixed upon the knife, hurling finally at society his cry of malediction. And, in spite of me, another spectacle rose suddenly before my mind. I saw a group of men and women pressing against each other in the middle of the oblong arena of the circus, under the gaze of thousands of eyes, while from all the steps of the immense amphitheatre went up the terrible cry, *Ad leones!* and, below, the opening cages of the wild beasts.

"I did not believe the execution would take place. In the first place, no victim had been struck with death, and it had long been the custom not to punish an abortive crime with the last degree of severity. Then, this crime, however terrible in intention, was disinterested, born of an abstract idea. The man's past, his abandoned childhood, his life of hardship, pleaded also in his favor. In the independent press generous voices were raised in his behalf, very loud and eloquent. 'A purely literary current of opinion' some have said, with no little scorn. *It is, on the contrary, an honor to the men of art and thought to have expressed once more their disgust at the scaffold.*"

Again Zola, in *Germinal* and *Paris,* describes the tenderness and kindness, the deep sympathy with human suffering, of these men who close the chapter of their lives with a violent outbreak against our system.

Last, but not least, the man who probably better than anyone else understands the psychology of the *Attentäter* is M. Hamon, the author of the brilliant work *Une Psychologie du Militaire Professionnel,* who has arrived at these suggestive conclusions:

"The positive method confirmed by the rational method enables us to establish an ideal type of Anarchist, whose mentality is the aggregate of common psychic characteristics. Every Anarchist partakes sufficiently of this ideal type to make it possible to differentiate him from other men. The typical Anarchist, then, may be defined as follows: A man perceptible by the spirit of revolt under one or more of its forms,—opposition, investigation, criticism, innovation,—endowed with a strong love of liberty, egoistic or individualistic, and possessed of great curiosity, a keen desire to know. These traits are supplemented by an ardent love of others, a highly developed moral sensitiveness, a profound sentiment of justice, and imbued with missionary zeal."

To the above characteristics, says Alvin F. Sanborn, must be added these sterling qualities: a rare love of animals, surpassing sweetness in all the ordinary relations of life, exceptional sobriety of demeanor, frugality and regularity, austerity, even, of living, and courage beyond compare.*

"There is a truism that the man in the street seems

---

* *Paris and the Social Revolution.*

always to forget, when he is abusing the Anarchists,
or whatever party happens to be his *bête noire* for the
moment, as the cause of some outrage just perpetrated. This indisputable fact is that homicidal outrages have, from time immemorial, been the reply of
goaded and desperate classes, and goaded and desperate individuals, to wrongs from their fellowmen,
which they felt to be intolerable. Such acts are the
violent recoil from violence, whether aggressive or
repressive; they are the last desperate struggle of outraged and exasperated human nature for breathing
space and life. And their cause lies not in any special
conviction, but in the depths of that human nature
itself. The whole course of history, political and
social, is strewn with evidence of this fact. To go no
further, take the three most notorious examples of
political parties goaded into violence during the last
fifty years: the Mazzinians in Italy, the Fenians in
Ireland, and the Terrorists in Russia. Were these
people Anarchists? No. Did they all three even
hold the same political opinions? No. The Mazzinians were Republicans, the Fenians political separa-
tists, the Russians Social Democrats or Constitutional-
ists. But all were driven by desperate circumstances
into this terrible form of revolt. And when we turn
from parties to individuals who have acted in like
manner, we stand appalled by the number of human
beings goaded and driven by sheer desperation into
conduct obviously violently opposed to their social
instincts.

"Now that Anarchism has become a living force in
society, such deeds have been sometimes committed

by Anarchists, as well as by others. For no new
faith, even the most essentially peaceable and humane
the mind of man has yet accepted, but at its first
coming has brought upon earth not peace, but a
sword; not because of anything violent or anti-social
in the doctrine itself; simply because of the ferment
any new and creative idea excites in men's minds,
whether they accept or reject it. And a conception of
Anarchism, which, on one hand, threatens every vested
interest, and, on the other, holds out a vision of a
free and noble life to be won by a struggle against
existing wrongs, is certain to rouse the fiercest opposition, and bring the whole repressive force of ancient
evil into violent contact with the tumultuous outburst
of a new hope.

"Under miserable conditions of life, any vision of
the possibility of better things makes the present misery more intolerable, and spurs those who suffer to
the most energetic struggles to improve their lot, and
if these struggles only immediately result in sharper
misery, the outcome is sheer desperation. In our
present society, for instance, an exploited wage
worker, who catches a glimpse of what work and life
might and ought to be, finds the toilsome routine and
the squalor of his existence almost intolerable; and
even when he has the resolution and courage to continue steadily working his best, and waiting until
new ideas have so permeated society as to pave the
way for better times, the mere fact that he has such
ideas and tries to spread them, brings him into difficulties with his employers. How many thousands of
Socialists, and above all Anarchists, have lost work

and even the chance of work, solely on the ground of
their opinions. It is only the specially gifted crafts-
man, who, if he be a zealous propagandist, can hope
to retain permanent employment. And what happens
to a man with his brain working actively with a
ferment of new ideas, with a vision before his eyes
of a new hope dawning for toiling and agonizing men,
with the knowledge that his suffering and that of his
fellows in misery is not caused by the cruelty of fate,
but by the injustice of other human beings,—what
happens to such a man when he sees those dear to
him starving, when he himself is starved? Some
natures in such a plight, and those by no means the
least social or the least sensitive, will become violent,
and will even feel that their violence is social and
not anti-social, that in striking when and how they
can, they are striking, not for themselves, but for
human nature, outraged and despoiled in their persons
and in those of their fellow sufferers. And are we,
who ourselves are not in this horrible predicament, to
stand by and coldly condemn these piteous victims of
the Furies and Fates? Are we to decry as miscreants
these human beings who act with heroic self-devotion,
sacrificing their lives in protest, where less social and
less energetic natures would lie down and grovel in
abject submission to injustice and wrong? Are we
to join the ignorant and brutal outcry which stig-
matizes such men as monsters of wickedness, gratu-
itously running amuck in a harmonious and innocently
peaceful society? No! We hate murder with a
hatred that may seem absurdly exaggerated to apologists for Matabele massacres, to callous acquiescers

in hangings and bombardments, but we decline in such cases of homicide, or attempted homicide, as those of which we are treating, to be guilty of the cruel injustice of flinging the whole responsibility of the deed upon the immediate perpetrator. The guilt of these homicides lies upon every man and woman who, intentionally or by cold indifference, helps to keep up social conditions that drive human beings to despair. The man who flings his whole life into the attempt, at the cost of his own life, to protest against the wrongs of his fellow men, is a saint compared to the active and passive upholders of cruelty and injustice, even if his protest destroy other lives besides his own. Let him who is without sin in society cast the first stone at such an one."*

That every act of political violence should nowadays be attributed to Anarchists is not at all surprising. Yet it is a fact known to almost everyone familiar with the Anarchist movement that a great number of acts, for which Anarchists had to suffer, either originated with the capitalist press or were instigated, if not directly perpetrated, by the police.

For a number of years acts of violence had been committed in Spain, for which the Anarchists were held responsible, hounded like wild beasts, and thrown into prison. Later it was disclosed that the perpetrators of these acts were not Anarchists, but members of the police department. The scandal became so widespread that the conservative Spanish papers demanded the apprehension and punishment of the

---

* From a pamphlet issued by the Freedom Group of London.

gang-leader, Juan Rull, who was subsequently condemned to death and executed. The sensational evidence, brought to light during the trial, forced Police Inspector Momento to exonerate completely the Anarchists from any connection with the acts committed during a long period. This resulted in the dismissal of a number of police officials, among them Inspector Tressols, who, in revenge, disclosed the fact that behind the gang of police bomb throwers were others of far higher position, who provided them with funds and protected them.

This is one of the many striking examples of how Anarchist conspiracies are manufactured.

That the American police can perjure themselves with the same ease, that they are just as merciless, just as brutal and cunning as their European colleagues, has been proven on more than one occasion. We need only recall the tragedy of the eleventh of November, 1887, known as the Haymarket Riot.

No one who is at all familiar with the case can possibly doubt that the Anarchists, judicially murdered in Chicago, died as victims of a lying, bloodthirsty press and of a cruel police conspiracy. Has not Judge Gary himself said: "Not because you have caused the Haymarket bomb, but because you are Anarchists, you are on trial."

The impartial and thorough analysis by Governor Altgeld of that blotch on the American escutcheon verified the brutal frankness of Judge Gary. It was this that induced Altgeld to pardon the three Anarchists, thereby earning the lasting esteem of every liberty-loving man and woman in the world.

When we approach the tragedy of September sixth, 1901, we are confronted by one of the most striking examples of how little social theories are responsible for an act of political violence. "Leon Czolgosz, an Anarchist, incited to commit the act by Emma Goldman." To be sure, has she not incited violence even before her birth, and will she not continue to do so beyond death? Everything is possible with the Anarchists.

Today, even, nine years after the tragedy, after it was proven a hundred times that Emma Goldman had nothing to do with the event, that no evidence whatsoever exists to indicate that Czolgosz ever called himself an Anarchist, we are confronted with the same lie, fabricated by the police and perpetuated by the press. No living soul ever heard Czolgosz make that statement, nor is there a single written word to prove that the boy ever breathed the accusation. Nothing but ignorance and insane hysteria, which have never yet been able to solve the simplest problem of cause and effect.

The President of a free Republic killed! What else can be the cause, except that the *Attentäter* must have been insane, or that he was incited to the act.

A free Republic! How a myth will maintain itself, how it will continue to deceive, to dupe, and blind even the comparatively intelligent to its monstrous absurdities. A free Republic! And yet within a little over thirty years a small band of parasites have successfully robbed the American people, and trampled upon the fundamental principles, laid down by the fathers of this country, guaranteeing to every man, woman, and child "life, liberty, and the pursuit of happiness." For thirty years they have been increasing their wealth and power at the expense of the vast mass of workers, thereby enlarging the army of the unemployed, the hungry, homeless, and friendless portion of humanity, who are tramping the country from east to west, from north to south, in a vain search for work. For many years the home has been left to the care of the little ones, while the parents are exhausting their life and strength for a mere pittance. For thirty years the sturdy sons of America have been sacrificed on the battlefield of industrial war, and the daughters outraged in corrupt factory surroundings. For long and weary years this process of undermining the nation's health, vigor, and pride, without much protest from the disinherited and oppressed, has been going on. Maddened by success and victory, the money powers of this "free land of ours" became more and more audacious in their heartless, cruel efforts to compete with the rotten and decayed European tyrannies for supremacy of power.

In vain did a lying press repudiate Leon Czolgosz as a foreigner. The boy was a product of our own free American soil, that lulled him to sleep with,

My country, 'tis of thee,
Sweet land of liberty.

Who can tell how many times this American child had gloried in the celebration of the Fourth of July, or of Decoration Day, when he faithfully honored the Nation's dead? Who knows but that he, too, was willing to "fight for his country and die for her liberty," until it dawned upon him that those he belonged to have no country, because they have been robbed of all that they have produced; until he realized that the liberty and independence of his youthful dreams were but a farce. Poor Leon Czolgosz, your crime consisted of too sensitive a social consciousness. Unlike your idealless and brainless American brothers, your ideals soared above the belly and the bank account. No wonder you impressed the one human being among all the infuriated mob at your trial— a newspaper woman—as a visionary, totally oblivious to your surroundings. Your large, dreamy eyes must have beheld a new and glorious dawn.

Now, to a recent instance of police-manufactured Anarchist plots. In that bloodstained city Chicago, the life of Chief of Police Shippy was attempted by a young man named Averbuch. Immediately the cry was sent to the four corners of the world that Averbuch was an Anarchist, and that the Anarchists were responsible for the act. Everyone who was at all known to entertain Anarchist ideas was closely watched, a number of people arrested, the library of an Anarchist group confiscated, and all meetings made impossible. It goes without saying that, as on various previous occasions, I must needs be held responsible for the act. Evidently the American police credit me with occult powers. I did not know Averbuch; in fact, had never before heard his name, and the only way I could have possibly "conspired" with him was in my astral body. But, then, the police are not concerned with logic or justice. What they seek is a target, to mask their absolute ignorance of the cause, of the psychology of a political act. Was Averbuch an Anarchist? There is no positive proof of it. He had been but three months in the country, did not know the language, and, as far as I could ascertain, was quite unknown to the Anarchists of Chicago.

What led to his act? Averbuch, like most young Russian immigrants, undoubtedly believed in the mythical liberty of America. He received his first baptism by the policeman's club during the brutal dispersement of the unemployed parade. He further experienced American equality and opportunity in the vain efforts to find an economic master. In short, a three months' sojourn in the glorious land brought him face to face with the fact that the disinherited are in the same position the world over. In his native land he probably learned that necessity knows no law —there was no difference between a Russian and an American policeman.

The question to the intelligent social student is not whether the acts of Czolgosz or Averbuch were practical, any more than whether the thunderstorm is practical. The thing that will inevitably impress itself on the thinking and feeling man and woman is that the sight of brutal clubbing of innocent victims in a so-called free Republic, and the degrading, soul-destroying economic struggle, furnish the spark that kindles the dynamic force in the overwrought, outraged souls of men like Czolgosz or Averbuch. No amount of persecution, of hounding, of repression, can stay this social phenomenon.

But, it is often asked, have not acknowledged Anarchists committed acts of violence? Certainly they have, always however ready to shoulder the responsibility. My contention is that they were impelled, not by the teachings of Anarchism, but by the tremendous pressure of conditions, making life unbearable to their sensitive natures. Obviously, Anarchism, or any other social theory, making man a conscious social unit, will act as a leaven for rebellion. This is not a mere assertion, but a fact verified by all experience. A close examination of the circumstances bearing upon this question will further clarify my position.

Let us consider some of the most important Anarchist acts within the last two decades. Strange as it may seem, one of the most significant deeds of political violence occurred here in America, in connection with the Homestead strike of 1892.

During that memorable time the Carnegie Steel Company organized a conspiracy to crush the Amalgamated Association of Iron and Steel Workers. Henry Clay Frick, then Chairman of the Company, was intrusted with that democratic task. He lost no time in carrying out the policy of breaking the Union, the policy which he had so successfully practiced during his reign of terror in the coke regions. Secretly, and while peace negotiations were being purposely prolonged, Frick supervised the military preparations, the fortification of the Homestead Steel Works, the erection of a high board fence, capped with barbed wire and provided with loopholes for sharpshooters. And then, in the dead of night, he attempted to smuggle his army of hired Pinkerton thugs into Homestead, which act precipitated the terrible carnage of the steel workers. Not content with the death of eleven victims, killed in the Pinkerton skirmish, Henry Clay Frick, good Christian and free American, straightway began the hounding down of the helpless wives and orphans, by ordering them out of the wretched Company houses.

The whole country was aroused over these inhuman outrages. Hundreds of voices were raised in protest, calling on Frick to desist, not to go too far. Yes, hundreds of people protested,—as one objects to annoying flies. Only one there was who actively responded to the outrage at Homestead,—Alexander Berkman. Yes, he was an Anarchist. He gloried in that fact, because it was the only force that made the discord between his spiritual longing and the world without at all bearable. Yet not Anarchism, as such, but the brutal slaughter of the eleven steel workers was the urge for Alexander Berkman's act, his attempt on the life of Henry Clay Frick.

The record of European acts of political violence affords numerous and striking instances of the influence of environment upon sensitive human beings.

The court speech of Vaillant, who, in 1894, exploded a bomb in the Paris Chamber of Deputies, strikes the true keynote of the psychology of such acts:

"Gentlemen, in a few minutes you are to deal your blow, but in receiving your verdict I shall have at least the satisfaction of having wounded the existing society, that cursed society in which one may see a single man spending, uselessly, enough to feed thousands of families; an infamous society which permits a few individuals to monopolize all the social wealth, while there are hundreds of thousands of unfortunates who have not even the bread that is not refused to dogs, and while entire families are committing suicide for want of the necessities of life.

"Ah, gentlemen, if the governing classes could go down among the unfortunates! But no, they prefer to remain deaf to their appeals. It seems that a fatality impels them, like the royalty of the eighteenth century, toward the precipice which will engulf them, for woe be to those who remain deaf to the cries of the starving, woe to those who, believing themselves of superior essence, assume the right to exploit those beneath them! There comes a time when the people no longer reason; they rise like a hurricane, and pass away like a torrent. Then we see bleeding heads impaled on pikes.

"Among the exploited, gentlemen, there are two classes of individuals. Those of one class, not realizing what they are and what they might be, take life as it comes, believe that they are born to be slaves, and content themselves with the little that is given them in exchange for their labor. But there are others, on the contrary, who think, who study, and who, looking about them, discover social iniquities. Is it their fault if they see clearly and suffer at seeing others suffer? Then they throw themselves into the struggle, and make themselves the bearers of the popular claims.

"Gentlemen, I am one of these last. Wherever I have gone, I have seen unfortunates bent beneath the yoke of capital. Everywhere I have seen the same

wounds causing tears of blood to flow, even in the
remoter parts of the inhabited districts of South
America, where I had the right to believe that he
who was weary of the pains of civilization might
rest in the shade of the palm trees and there study
nature. Well, there even, more than elsewhere, I
have seen capital come, like a vampire, to suck the
last drop of blood of the unfortunate pariahs.

"Then I came back to France, where it was re-
served for me to see my family suffer atrociously.
This was the last drop in the cup of my sorrow.
Tired of leading this life of suffering and cowardice, I carried this bomb to those who are primarily
responsible for social misery.

"I am reproached with the wounds of those who
were hit by my projectiles. Permit me to point out
in passing that, if the bourgeois had not massacred
or caused massacres during the Revolution, it is
probable that they would still be under the yoke of
the nobility. On the other hand, figure up the dead
and wounded of Tonquin, Madagascar, Dahomey,
adding thereto the thousands, yes, millions of unfortunates who die in the factories, the mines, and
wherever the grinding power of capital is felt. Add
also those who die of hunger, and all this with the
assent of our Deputies. Beside all this, of how little
weight are the reproaches now brought against me!

"It is true that one does not efface the other; but,
after all, are we not acting on the defensive when
we respond to the blows which we receive from
above? I know very well that I shall be told that I
ought to have confined myself to speech for the

vindication of the people's claims. But what can you expect! It takes a loud voice to make the deaf hear. Too long have they answered our voices by imprisonment, the rope, rifle volleys. Make no mistake; the explosion of my bomb is not only the cry of the rebel Vaillant, but the cry of an entire class which vindicates its rights, and which will soon add acts to words. For, be sure of it, in vain will they pass laws. The ideas of the thinkers will not halt; just as, in the last century, all the governmental forces could not prevent the Diderots and the Voltaires from spreading emancipating ideas among the people, so all the existing governmental forces will not prevent the Reclus, the Darwins, the Spencers, the Ibsens, the Mirbeaus, from spreading the ideas of justice and liberty which will annihilate the prejudices that hold the mass in ignorance. And these ideas, welcomed by the unfortunate, will flower in acts of revolt as they have done in me, until the day when the disappearance of authority shall permit all men to organize freely according to their choice, when everyone shall be able to enjoy the product of his labor, and when those moral maladies called prejudices shall vanish, permitting human beings to live in harmony, having no other desire than to study the sciences and love their fellows.

"I conclude, gentlemen, by saying that a society in which one sees such social inequalities as we see all about us, in which we see every day suicides caused by poverty, prostitution flaring at every street corner, —a society whose principal monuments are barracks and prisons,—such a society must be transformed as soon as possible, on pain of being eliminated, and that speedily, from the human race. Hail to him who labors, by no matter what means, for this transformation! It is this idea that has guided me in my duel with authority, but as in this duel I have only wounded my adversary, it is now its turn to strike me.

"Now, gentlemen, to me it matters little what penalty you may inflict, for, looking at this assembly with the eyes of reason, I can not help smiling to see you, atoms lost in matter, and reasoning only because you possess a prolongation of the spinal marrow, assume the right to judge one of your fellows.

"Ah! gentlemen, how little a thing is your assembly and your verdict in the history of humanity; and human history, in its turn, is likewise a very little thing in the whirlwind which bears it through immensity, and which is destined to disappear, or at least to be transformed, in order to begin again the same history and the same facts, a veritably perpetual play of cosmic forces renewing and transferring themselves forever."

Will anyone say that Vaillant was an ignorant, vicious man, or a lunatic? Was not his mind singularly clear and analytic? No wonder that the best intellectual forces of France spoke in his behalf, and signed the petition to President Carnot, asking him to commute Vaillant's death sentence.

Carnot would listen to no entreaty; he insisted on more than a pound of flesh, he wanted Vaillant's life, and then—the inevitable happened: President

Carnot was killed. On the handle of the stiletto used by the *Attentäter* was engraved, significantly,

VAILLANT!

Santa Caserio was an Anarchist. He could have gotten away, saved himself; but he remained, he stood the consequences.

His reasons for the act are set forth in so simple, dignified, and childlike manner that one is reminded of the touching tribute paid Caserio by his teacher of the little village school, Ada Negri, the Italian poet, who spoke of him as a sweet, tender plant, of too fine and sensitive texture to stand the cruel strain of the world.

"Gentlemen of the Jury! I do not propose to make a defense, but only an explanation of my deed.

"Since my early youth I began to learn that present society is badly organized, so badly that every day many wretched men commit suicide, leaving women and children in the most terrible distress. Workers, by thousands, seek for work and can not find it. Poor families beg for food and shiver with cold; they suffer the greatest misery; the little ones ask their miserable mothers for food, and the mothers cannot give it to them, because they have nothing. The few things which the home contained have already been sold or pawned. All they can do is beg alms; often they are arrested as vagabonds.

"I went away from my native place because I was frequently moved to tears at seeing little girls of eight or ten years obliged to work fifteen hours a day for the paltry pay of twenty centimes. Young women of eighteen or twenty also work fifteen hours daily, for a mockery of remuneration. And that happens not only to my fellow countrymen, but to all the workers, who sweat the whole day long for a crust of bread, while their labor produces wealth in abundance. The workers are obliged to live under the most wretched conditions, and their food consists of a little bread, a few spoonfuls of rice, and water; so by the time they are thirty or forty years old, they are exhausted, and go to die in the hospitals. Besides, in consequence of bad food and overwork, these unhappy creatures are, by hundreds, devoured by pellagra—a disease that, in my country, attacks, as the physicians say, those who are badly fed and lead a life of toil and privation.

"I have observed that there are a great many people who are hungry, and many children who suffer, whilst bread and clothes abound in the towns. I saw many and large shops full of clothing and woolen stuffs, and I also saw warehouses full of wheat and Indian corn, suitable for those who are in want. And, on the other hand, I saw thousands of people who do not work, who produce nothing and live on the labor of others; who spend every day thousands of francs for their amusement; who debauch the daughters of the workers; who own dwellings of forty or fifty rooms; twenty or thirty horses, many servants; in a word, all the pleasures of life.

"I believed in God; but when I saw so great an inequality between men, I acknowledged that it was not God who created man, but man who created God. And I discovered that those who want their property to be respected, have an interest in preaching the existence of paradise and hell, and in keeping the people in ignorance.

"Not long ago, Vaillant threw a bomb in the Chamber of Deputies, to protest against the present system of society. He killed no one, only wounded some persons; yet bourgeois justice sentenced him to death. And not satisfied with the condemnation of the guilty man, they began to pursue the Anarchists, and arrest not only those who had known Vaillant, but even those who had merely been present at any Anarchist lecture.

"The government did not think of their wives and children. It did not consider that the men kept in prison were not the only ones who suffered, and that their little ones cried for bread. Bourgeois justice did not trouble itself about these innocent ones, who do not yet know what society is. It is no fault of theirs that their fathers are in prison; they only want to eat.

"The government went on searching private houses, opening private letters, forbidding lectures and meetings, and practicing the most infamous oppressions against us. Even now, hundreds of Anarchists are arrested for having written an article in a newspaper, or for having expressed an opinion in public.

"Gentlemen of the Jury, you are representatives of bourgeois society. If you want my head, take it; but do not believe that in so doing you will stop the Anarchist propaganda. Take care, for men reap what they have sown."

During a religious procession in 1896, at Barcelona, a bomb was thrown. Immediately three hundred men and women were arrested. Some were Anarchists, but the majority were trade-unionists and Socialists. They were thrown into that terrible bastille Montjuich, and subjected to most horrible tortures. After a number had been killed, or had gone insane, their cases were taken up by the liberal press of Europe, resulting in the release of a few survivors.

The man primarily responsible for this revival of the Inquisition was Canovas del Castillo, Prime Minister of Spain. It was he who ordered the torturing of the victims, their flesh burned, their bones crushed, their tongues cut out. Practiced in the art of brutality during his régime in Cuba, Canovas remained absolutely deaf to the appeals and protests of the awakened civilized conscience.

In 1897 Canovas del Castillo was shot to death by a young Italian, Angiolillo. The latter was an editor in his native land, and his bold utterances soon attracted the attention of the authorities. Persecution began, and Angiolillo fled from Italy to Spain, thence to France and Belgium, finally settling in England. While there he found employment as a compositor, and immediately became the friend of all his colleagues. One of the latter thus described Angiolillo: "His appearance suggested the journalist rather than the disciple of Guttenberg. His delicate hands, moreover, betrayed the fact that he had not grown up at the 'case.' With his handsome frank face, his soft dark hair, his alert expression, he looked the very type of the vivacious Southerner.

Angiolillo spoke Italian, Spanish, and French, but no English; the little French I knew was not sufficient to carry on a prolonged conversation. However, Angiolillo soon began to acquire the English idiom; he learned rapidly, playfully, and it was not long until he became very popular with his fellow compositors. His distinguished and yet modest manner, and his consideration towards his colleagues, won him the hearts of all the boys."

Angiolillo soon became familiar with the detailed accounts in the press. He read of the great wave of human sympathy with the helpless victims at Montjuich. On Trafalgar Square he saw with his own eyes the results of those atrocities, when the few Spaniards, who escaped Castillo's clutches, came to seek asylum in England. There, at the great meeting, these men opened their shirts and showed the horrible scars of burned flesh. Angiolillo saw, and the effect surpassed a thousand theories; the impetus was beyond words, beyond arguments, beyond himself even.

Señor Antonio Canovas del Castillo, Prime Minister of Spain, sojourned at Santa Agueda. As usual in such cases, all strangers were kept away from his exalted presence. One exception was made, however, in the case of a distinguished looking, elegantly dressed Italian—the representative, it was understood, of an important journal. The distinguished gentleman was—Angiolillo.

Señor Canovas, about to leave his house, stepped on the veranda. Suddenly Angiolillo confronted him. A shot rang out, and Canovas was a corpse.

The wife of the Prime Minister rushed upon the scene. "Murderer! Murderer!" she cried, pointing at Angiolillo. The latter bowed. "Pardon, Madame," he said, "I respect you as a lady, but I regret that you were the wife of that man."

Calmly Angiolillo faced death. Death in its most terrible form—for the man whose soul was as a child's.

He was garroted. His body lay, sun-kissed, till the day hid in twilight. And the people came, and pointing the finger of terror and fear, they said: "There—the criminal—the cruel murderer."

How stupid, how cruel is ignorance! It misunderstands always, condemns always.

A remarkable parallel to the case of Angiolillo is to be found in the act of Gaetano Bresci, whose *Attentat* upon King Umberto made an American city famous.

Bresci came to this country, this land of opportunity, where one has but to try to meet with golden success. Yes, he too would try to succeed. He would work hard and faithfully. Work had no terrors for him, if it would only help him to independence, manhood, self-respect.

Thus full of hope and enthusiasm he settled in Paterson, New Jersey, and there found a lucrative job at six dollars per week in one of the weaving mills of the town. Six whole dollars per week was, no doubt, a fortune for Italy, but not enough to breathe on in the new country. He loved his little home. He was a good husband and devoted father to his *bambina* Bianca, whom he adored. He worked and worked

for a number of years. He actually managed to save
one hundred dollars out of his six dollars per week.

Bresci had an ideal. Foolish, I know, for a workingman to have an ideal,—the Anarchist paper published in Paterson, *La Questione Sociale*.

Every week, though tired from work, he would
help to set up the paper. Until late hours he would
assist, and when the little pioneer had exhausted all
resources and his comrades were in despair, Bresci
brought cheer and hope, one hundred dollars, the
entire savings of years. That would keep the paper
afloat.

In his native land people were starving. The
crops had been poor, and the peasants saw themselves
face to face with famine. They appealed to their
good King Umberto; he would help. And he did.
The wives of the peasants who had gone to the palace
of the King, held up in mute silence their emaciated
infants. Surely that would move him. And then
the soldiers fired and killed those poor fools.

Bresci, at work in the weaving mill at Paterson,
read of the horrible massacre. His mental eye beheld
the defenceless women and innocent infants of his
native land, slaughtered right before the good King.
His soul recoiled in horror. At night he heard the
groans of the wounded. Some may have been his
comrades, his own flesh. Why, why these foul
murders?

The little meeting of the Italian Anarchist group
in Paterson ended almost in a fight. Bresci had demanded his hundred dollars. His comrades begged,
implored him to give them a respite. The paper

would go down if they were to return him his loan. But Bresci insisted on its return.

How cruel and stupid is ignorance. Bresci got the money, but lost the good will, the confidence of his comrades. They would have nothing more to do with one whose greed was greater than his ideals.

On the twenty-ninth of July, 1900, King Umberto was shot at Monzo. The young Italian weaver of Paterson, Gaetano Bresci, had taken the life of the good King.

Paterson was placed under police surveillance, everyone known as an Anarchist hounded and persecuted, and the act of Bresci ascribed to the teachings of Anarchism. As if the teachings of Anarchism in its extremest form could equal the force of those slain women and infants, who had pilgrimed to the King for aid. As if any spoken word, ever so eloquent, could burn into a human soul with such white heat as the lifeblood trickling drop by drop from those dying forms. The ordinary man is rarely moved either by word or deed; and those whose social kinship is the greatest living force need no appeal to respond—even as does steel to the magnet —to the wrongs and horrors of society.

If a social theory is a strong factor inducing acts of political violence, how are we to account for the recent violent outbreaks in India, where Anarchism has hardly been born. More than any other old philosophy, Hindu teachings have exalted passive resistance, the drifting of life, the Nirvana, as the highest spiritual ideal. Yet the social unrest in India is daily growing, and has only recently resulted in an act of political violence, the killing of Sir Curzon Wyllie by the Hindu Madar Sol Dhingra.

If such a phenomenon can occur in a country socially and individually permeated for centuries with the spirit of passivity, can one question the tremendous, revolutionizing effect on human character exerted by great social iniquities? Can one doubt the logic, the justice of these words:

"Repression, tyranny, and indiscriminate punishment of innocent men have been the watchwords of the government of the alien domination in India ever since we began the commercial boycott of English goods. The tiger qualities of the British are much in evidence now in India. They think that by the strength of the sword they will keep down India! It is this arrogance that has brought about the bomb, and the more they tyrannize over a helpless and unarmed people, the more terrorism will grow. We may deprecate terrorism as outlandish and foreign to our culture, but it is inevitable as long as this tyranny continues, for it is not the terrorists that are to be blamed, but the tyrants who are responsible for it. It is the only resource for a helpless and unarmed people when brought to the verge of despair. It is never criminal on their part. The crime lies with the tyrant."*

Even conservative scientists are beginning to realize that heredity is not the sole factor moulding human character. Climate, food, occupation; nay,

---

* *The Free Hindustan.*

color, light, and sound must be considered in the study of human psychology.

If that be true, how much more correct is the contention that great social abuses will and must influence different minds and temperaments in a different way. And how utterly fallacious the stereotyped notion that the teachings of Anarchism, or certain exponents of these teachings, are responsible for the acts of political violence.

Anarchism, more than any other social theory, values human life above things. All Anarchists agree with Tolstoy in this fundamental truth: if the production of any commodity necessitates the sacrifice of human life, society should do without that commodity, but it can not do without that life. That, however, nowise indicates that Anarchism teaches submission. How can it, when it knows that all suffering, all misery, all ills, result from the evil of submission?

Has not some American ancestor said, many years ago, that resistance to tyranny is obedience to God? And he was not an Anarchist even. I would say that resistance to tyranny is man's highest ideal. So long as tyranny exists, in whatever form, man's deepest aspiration must resist it as inevitably as man must breathe.

Compared with the wholesale violence of capital and government, political acts of violence are but a drop in the ocean. That so few resist is the strongest proof how terrible must be the conflict between their souls and unbearable social iniquities.

High strung, like a violin string, they weep and moan for life, so relentless, so cruel, so terribly inhuman.   In a desperate moment the string breaks. Untuned ears hear nothing but discord.   But those who feel the agonized cry understand its harmony; they hear in it the fulfillment of the most compelling moment of human nature.

Such is the psychology of political violence.

PRISONS

A SOCIAL CRIME AND FAILURE

IN 1849 Feodor Dostoyevsky wrote on the wall of his prison cell the following story of *The Priest and the Devil:*

" 'Hello, you little fat father!' the devil said to the priest. 'What made you lie so to those poor, misled people? What tortures of hell did you depict? Don't you know they are already suffering the tortures of hell in their earthly lives? Don't you know that you and the authorities of the State are my representatives on earth? It is you that make them suffer the pains of hell with which you threaten them. Don't you know this? Well, then, come with me!'

"The devil grabbed the priest by the collar, lifted him high in the air, and carried him to a factory, to an iron foundry. He saw the workmen there running and hurrying to and fro, and toiling in the scorching heat. Very soon the thick, heavy air and the heat are too much for the priest. With tears in his eyes, he pleads with the devil: 'Let me go! Let me leave this hell!'

" 'Oh, my dear friend, I must show you many more

places.' The devil gets hold of him again and drags him off to a farm. There he sees workmen threshing the grain. The dust and heat are insufferable. The overseer carries a knout, and unmercifully beats any-one who falls to the ground overcome by hard toil or hunger.

"Next the priest is taken to the huts where these same workers live with their families—dirty, cold, smoky, ill-smelling holes. The devil grins. He points out the poverty and hardships which are at home here.

" 'Well, isn't this enough?' he asks. And it seems as if even he, the devil, pities the people. The pious servant of God can hardly bear it. With uplifted hands he begs: 'Let me go away from here. Yes, yes! This is hell on earth!'

" 'Well, then, you see. And you still promise them another hell. You torment them, torture them to death mentally when they are already all but dead physically! Come on! I will show you one more hell—one more, the very worst.'

"He took him to a prison and showed him a dungeon, with its foul air and the many human forms, robbed of all health and energy, lying on the floor, covered with vermin that were devouring their poor, naked, emaciated bodies.

" 'Take off your silken clothes,' said the devil to the priest, 'put on your ankles heavy chains such as these unfortunates wear; lie down on the cold and filthy floor—and then talk to them about a hell that still awaits them!'

" 'No, no!' answered the priest, 'I cannot think of

anything more dreadful than this. I entreat you, let me go away from here!'

" 'Yes, this is hell. There can be no worse hell than this. Did you not know it? Did you not know that these men and women whom you are frightening with the picture of a hell hereafter—did you not know that they are in hell right here, before they die?"

This was written fifty years ago in dark Russia, on the wall of one of the most horrible prisons. Yet who can deny that the same applies with equal force to the present time, even to American prisons?

With all our boasted reforms, our great social changes, and our far-reaching discoveries, human beings continue to be sent to the worst of hells, wherein they are outraged, degraded, and tortured, that society may be "protected" from the phantoms of its own making.

Prison, a social protection? What monstrous mind ever conceived such an idea? Just as well say that health can be promoted by a widespread contagion.

After eighteen months of horror in an English prison, Oscar Wilde gave to the world his great masterpiece, *The Ballad of Reading Goal:*

> The vilest deeds, like poison weeds,
>   Bloom well in prison air;
> It is only what is good in Man
>   That wastes and withers there.
> Pale Anguish keeps the heavy gate,
>   And the Warder is Despair.

Society goes on perpetuating this poisonous air, not realizing that out of it can come naught but the most poisonous results.

We are spending at the present $3,500,000 per day, $1,000,095,000 per year, to maintain prison institutions, and that in a democratic country,—a sum almost as large as the combined output of wheat, valued at $750,000,000, and the output of coal, valued at $350,000,000. Professor Bushnell of Washington, D. C., estimates the cost of prisons at $6,000,000,000 annually, and Dr. G. Frank Lydston, an eminent American writer on crime, gives $5,000,000,000 annually as a reasonable figure. Such unheard-of expenditure for the purpose of maintaining vast armies of human beings caged up like wild beasts!*

Yet crimes are on the increase. Thus we learn that in America there are four and a half times as many crimes to every million population today as there were twenty years ago.

The most horrible aspect is that our national crime is murder, not robbery, embezzlement, or rape, as in the South. London is five times as large as Chicago, yet there are one hundred and eighteen murders annually in the latter city, while only twenty in London. Nor is Chicago the leading city in crime, since it is only seventh on the list, which is headed by four Southern cities, and San Francisco and Los Angeles. In view of such a terrible condition of affairs, it seems ridiculous to prate of the protection society derives from its prisons.

---

* *Crime and Criminals.* W. C. Owen.

The average mind is slow in grasping a truth, but when the most thoroughly organized, centralized institution, maintained at an excessive national expense, has proven a complete social failure, the dullest must begin to question its right to exist. The time is past when we can be content with our social fabric merely because it is "ordained by divine right," or by the majesty of the law.

The widespread prison investigations, agitation, and education during the last few years are conclusive proof that men are learning to dig deep into the very bottom of society, down to the causes of the terrible discrepancy between social and individual life.

Why, then, are prisons a social crime and a failure? To answer this vital question it behooves us to seek the nature and cause of crimes, the methods employed in coping with them, and the effects these methods produce in ridding society of the curse and horror of crimes.

First, as to the *nature* of crime:

Havelock Ellis divides crime into four phases, the political, the passional, the insane, and the occasional. He says that the political criminal is the victim of an attempt of a more or less despotic government to preserve its own stability. He is not necessarily guilty of an unsocial offense; he simply tries to overturn a certain political order which may itself be anti-social. This truth is recognized all over the world, except in America where the foolish notion still prevails that in a Democracy there is no place for political criminals. Yet John Brown was a political criminal; so were the Chicago Anarchists; so is every striker. Consequently, says Havelock Ellis, the political criminal of our time or place may be the hero, martyr, saint of another age. Lombroso calls the political criminal the true precursor of the progressive movement of humanity.

"The criminal by passion is usually a man of wholesome birth and honest life, who under the stress of some great, unmerited wrong has wrought justice for himself."*

Mr. Hugh C. Weir, in *The Menace of the Police,* cites the case of Jim Flaherty, a criminal by passion, who, instead of being saved by society, is turned into a drunkard and a recidivist, with a ruined and poverty-stricken family as the result.

A more pathetic type is Archie, the victim in Brand Whitlock's novel, *The Turn of the Balance,* the greatest American exposé of crime in the making. Archie, even more than Flaherty, was driven to crime and death by the cruel inhumanity of his surroundings, and by the unscrupulous hounding of the machinery of the law. Archie and Flaherty are but the types of many thousands, demonstrating how the legal aspects of crime, and the methods of dealing with it, help to create the disease which is undermining our entire social life.

"The insane criminal really can no more be considered a criminal than a child, since he is mentally in the same condition as an infant or an animal."*

The law already recognizes that, but only in rare cases of a very flagrant nature, or when the culprit's

---

* *The Criminal,* Havelock Ellis.

wealth permits the luxury of criminal insanity. It has become quite fashionable to be the victim of paranoia. But on the whole the "sovereignty of justice" still continues to punish criminally insane with the whole severity of its power. Thus Mr. Ellis quotes from Dr. Richter's statistics showing that in Germany one hundred and six madmen, out of one hundred and forty-four criminally insane, were condemned to severe punishment.

The occasional criminal "represents by far the largest class of our prison population, hence is the greatest menace to social well-being." What is the cause that compels a vast army of the human family to take to crime, to prefer the hideous life within prison walls to the life outside? Certainly that cause must be an iron master, who leaves its victims no avenue of escape, for the most depraved human being loves liberty.

This terrific force is conditioned in our cruel social and economic arrangement. I do not mean to deny the biologic, physiologic, or psychologic factors in creating crime; but there is hardly an advanced criminologist who will not concede that the social and economic influences are the most relentless, the most poisonous germs of crime. Granted even that there are innate criminal tendencies, it is none the less true that these tendencies find rich nutrition in our social environment.

There is close relation, says Havelock Ellis, between crimes against the person and the price of alcohol, between crimes against property and the price of wheat. He quotes Quetelet and Lacassagne, the former looking upon society as the preparer of crime, and the criminals as instruments that execute them. The latter finds that "the social environment is the cultivation medium of criminality; that the criminal is the microbe, an element which only becomes important when it finds the medium which causes it to ferment; *every society has the criminals it deserves.*"*

The most "prosperous" industrial period makes it impossible for the worker to earn enough to keep up health and vigor. And as prosperity is, at best, an imaginary condition, thousands of people are constantly added to the host of the unemployed. From East to West, from South to North, this vast army tramps in search of work or food, and all they find is the workhouse or the slums. Those who have a spark of self-respect left, prefer open defiance, prefer crime to the emaciated, degraded position of poverty.

Edward Carpenter estimates that five-sixths of indictable crimes consist in some violation of property rights; but that is too low a figure. A thorough investigation would prove that nine crimes out of ten could be traced, directly or indirectly, to our economic and social iniquities, to our system of remorseless exploitation and robbery. There is no criminal so stupid but recognizes this terrible fact, though he may not be able to account for it.

A collection of criminal philosophy, which Havelock Ellis, Lombroso, and other eminent men have compiled, shows that the criminal feels only too

---

* *The Criminal.*

keenly that it is society that drives him to crime. A Milanese thief said to Lombroso: "I do not rob, I merely take from the rich their superfluities; besides, do not advocates and merchants rob?" A murderer wrote: "Knowing that three-fourths of the social virtues are cowardly vices, I thought an open assault on a rich man would be less ignoble than the cautious combination of fraud." Another wrote: "I am imprisoned for stealing a half dozen eggs. Ministers who rob millions are honored. Poor Italy!" An educated convict said to Mr. Davitt: "The laws of society are framed for the purpose of securing the wealth of the world to power and calculation, thereby depriving the larger portion of mankind of its rights and chances. Why should they punish me for taking by somewhat similar means from those who have taken more than they had a right to?" The same man added: "Religion robs the soul of its independence; patriotism is the stupid worship of the world for which the well-being and the peace of the inhabitants were sacrificed by those who profit by it, while the laws of the land, in restraining natural desires, were waging war on the manifest spirit of the law of our beings. Compared with this," he concluded, "thieving is an honorable pursuit."*

Verily, there is greater truth in this philosophy than in all the law-and-moral books of society.

The economic, political, moral, and physical factors being the microbes of crime, how does society meet the situation?

---

* *The Criminal.*

The methods of coping with crime have no doubt undergone several changes, but mainly in a theoretic sense. In practice, society has retained the primitive motive in dealing with the offender; that is, revenge. It has also adopted the theologic idea; namely, punishment; while the legal and "civilized" methods consist of deterrence or terror, and reform. We shall presently see that all four modes have failed utterly, and that we are today no nearer a solution than in the dark ages.

The natural impulse of the primitive man to strike back, to avenge a wrong, is out of date. Instead, the civilized man, stripped of courage and daring, has delegated to an organized machinery the duty of avenging his wrongs, in the foolish belief that the State is justified in doing what he no longer has the manhood or consistency to do. The "majesty of the law" is a reasoning thing; it would not stoop to primitive instincts. Its mission is of a "higher" nature. True, it is still steeped in the theologic muddle, which proclaims punishment as a means of purification, or the vicarious atonement of sin. But legally and socially the statute exercises punishment, not merely as an infliction of pain upon the offender, but also for its terrifying effect upon others.

What is the real basis of punishment, however? The notion of a free will, the idea that man is at all times a free agent for good or evil; if he chooses the latter, he must be made to pay the price. Although this theory has long been exploded, and thrown upon the dustheap, it continues to be applied daily by the entire machinery of government, turning it into the

most cruel and brutal tormentor of human life. The
only reason for its continuance is the still more cruel
notion that the greater the terror punishment spreads,
the more certain its preventative effect.

Society is using the most drastic methods in dealing with the social offender. Why do they not deter?
Although in America a man is supposed to be considered innocent until proven guilty, the instruments
of law, the police, carry on a reign of terror, making
indiscriminate arrests, beating, clubbing, bullying
people, using the barbarous method of the "third
degree," subjecting their unfortunate victims to the
foul air of the station house, and the still fouler language of its guardians. Yet crimes are rapidly multiplying, and society is paying the price. On the other
hand, it is an open secret that when the unfortunate
citizen has been given the full "mercy" of the law,
and for the sake of safety is hidden in the worst of
hells, his real Calvary begins. Robbed of his rights as
a human being, degraded to a mere automaton without will or feeling, dependent entirely upon the mercy
of brutal keepers, he daily goes through a process of
dehumanization, compared with which savage revenge
was mere child's play.

There is not a single penal institution or reformatory in the United States where men are not tortured
"to be made good," by means of the black-jack, the
club, the strait-jacket, the water-cure, the "hum-
ming bird" (an electrical contrivance run along the
human body), the solitary, the bull-ring, and starvation diet. In these institutions his will is broken, his
soul degraded, his spirit subdued by the deadly mo-

notony and routine of prison life. In Ohio, Illinois, Pennsylvania, Missouri, and in the South, these horrors have become so flagrant as to reach the outside world, while in most other prisons the same Christian methods still prevail. But prison walls rarely allow the agonized shrieks of the victims to escape—prison walls are thick, they dull the sound. Society might with greater immunity abolish all prisons at once, than to hope for protection from these twentieth-century chambers of horrors.

Year after year the gates of prison hells return to the world an emaciated, deformed, will-less, shipwrecked crew of humanity, with the Cain mark on their foreheads, their hopes crushed, all their natural inclinations thwarted. With nothing but hunger and inhumanity to greet them, these victims soon sink back into crime as the only possibility of existence. It is not at all an unusual thing to find men and women who have spent half their lives—nay, almost their entire existence—in prison. I know a woman on Blackwell's Island, who had been in and out thirty-eight times; and through a friend I learn that a young boy of seventeen, whom he had nursed and cared for in the Pittsburg penitentiary, had never known the meaning of liberty. From the reformatory to the penitentiary had been the path of this boy's life, until, broken in body, he died a victim of social revenge. These personal experiences are substantiated by extensive data giving overwhelming proof of the utter futility of prisons as a means of deterrence or reform.

Well-meaning persons are now working for a new departure in the prison question,—reclamation, to

restore once more to the prisoner the possibility of
becoming a human being. Commendable as this is, I
fear it is impossible to hope for good results from
pouring good wine into a musty bottle. Nothing
short of a complete reconstruction of society will
deliver mankind from the cancer of crime. Still, if
the dull edge of our social conscience would be sharp-
ened, the penal institutions might be given a new coat
of varnish. But the first step to be taken is the
renovation of the social consciousness, which is in a
rather dilapidated condition. It is sadly in need to
be awakened to the fact that crime is a question of
degree, that we all have the rudiments of crime in us,
more or less, according to our mental, physical, and
social environment; and that the individual criminal
is merely a reflex of the tendencies of the aggregate.

With the social consciousness wakened, the average individual may learn to refuse the "honor" of
being the bloodhound of the law. He may cease to
persecute, despise, and mistrust the social offender,
and give him a chance to live and breathe among his
fellows. Institutions are, of course, harder to reach.
They are cold, impenetrable, and cruel; still, with the
social consciousness quickened, it might be possible to
free the prison victims from the brutality of prison
officials, guards, and keepers. Public opinion is a
powerful weapon; keepers of human prey, even, are
afraid of it. They may be taught a little humanity,
especially if they realize that their jobs depend upon it.

But the most important step is to demand for the
prisoner the right to work while in prison, with some
monetary recompense that would enable him to lay

aside a little for the day of his release, the beginning of a new life.

It is almost ridiculous to hope much from present society when we consider that workingmen, wage-slaves themselves, object to convict labor. I shall not go into the cruelty of this objection, but merely consider the impracticability of it. To begin with, the opposition so far raised by organized labor has been directed against windmills. Prisoners have always worked; only the State has been their exploiter, even as the individual employer has been the robber of organized labor. The States have either set the convicts to work for the government, or they have farmed convict labor to private individuals. Twenty-nine of the States pursue the latter plan. The Federal government and seventeen States have discarded it, as have the leading nations of Europe, since it leads to hideous overworking and abuse of prisoners, and to endless graft.

"Rhode Island, the State dominated by Aldrich, offers perhaps the worst example. Under a five-year contract, dated July 7th, 1906, and renewable for five years more at the option of private contractors, the labor of the inmates of the Rhode Island Penitentiary and the Providence County Jail is sold to the Reliance-Sterling Mfg. Co. at the rate of a trifle less than 25 cents a day per man. This Company is really a gigantic Prison Labor Trust, for it also leases the convict labor of Connecticut, Michigan, Indiana, Nebraska, and South Dakota penitentiaries, and the reformatories of New Jersey, Indiana, Illinois, and Wisconsin, eleven establishments in all.

"The enormity of the graft under the Rhode Island contract may be estimated from the fact that this same Company pays 62½ cents a day in Nebraska for the convict's labor, and that Tennessee, for example, gets $1.10 a day for a convict's work from the Gray-Dudley Hardware Co.; Missouri gets 70 cents a day from the Star Overall Mfg. Co.; West Virginia 65 cents a day from the Kraft Mfg. Co., and Maryland 55 cents a day from Oppenheim, Oberndorf & Co., shirt manufacturers. The very difference in prices points to enormous graft. For example, the Reliance-Sterling Mfg. Co. manufactures shirts, the cost by free labor being not less than $1.20 per dozen, while it pays Rhode Island thirty cents a dozen. Furthermore, the State charges this Trust no rent for the use of its huge factory, charges nothing for power, heat, light, or even drainage, and exacts no taxes. What graft!"*

It is estimated that more than twelve million dollars' worth of workingmen's shirts and overalls is produced annually in this country by prison labor. It is a woman's industry, and the first reflection that arises is that an immense amount of free female labor is thus displaced. The second consideration is that male convicts, who should be learning trades that would give them some chance of being self-supporting after their release, are kept at this work at which they can not possibly make a dollar. This is the more serious when we consider that much of this labor is done in reformatories, which so loudly profess to be training their inmates to become useful citizens.

---

* Quoted from the publications of the National Committee on Prison Labor.

The third, and most important, consideration is that the enormous profits thus wrung from convict labor are a constant incentive to the contractors to exact from their unhappy victims tasks altogether beyond their strength, and to punish them cruelly when their work does not come up to the excessive demands made.

Another word on the condemnation of convicts to tasks at which they cannot hope to make a living after release. Indiana, for example, is a State that has made a great splurge over being in the front rank of modern penological improvements. Yet, according to the report rendered in 1908 by the training school of its "reformatory," 135 were engaged in the manufacture of chains, 207 in that of shirts, and 255 in the foundry—a total of 597 in three occupations. But at this so-called reformatory 59 occupations were represented by the inmates, 39 of which were connected with country pursuits. Indiana, like other States, professes to be training the inmates of her reformatory to occupations by which they will be able to make their living when released. She actually sets them to work making chains, shirts, and brooms, the latter for the benefit of the Louisville Fancy Grocery Co. Broom-making is a trade largely monopolized by the blind, shirt-making is done by women, and there is only one free chain-factory in the State, and at that a released convict can not hope to get employment. The whole thing is a cruel farce.

If, then, the States can be instrumental in robbing their helpless victims of such tremendous profits is it not high time for organized labor to stop its idle howl;

and to insist on decent remuneration for the convict,
even as labor organizations claim for themselves? In
that way workingmen would kill the germ which
makes of the prisoner an enemy to the interests of
labor. I have said elsewhere that thousands of convicts, incompetent and without a trade, without means
of subsistence, are yearly turned back into the social
fold. These men and women must live, for even an
ex-convict has needs. Prison life has made them
anti-social beings, and the rigidly closed doors that
meet them on their release are not likely to decrease
their bitterness. The inevitable result is that they
form a favorable nucleus out of which scabs, black-
legs, detectives, and policemen are drawn, only too
willing to do the master's bidding. Thus organized
labor, by its foolish opposition to work in prison,
defeats its own ends. It helps to create poisonous
fumes that stifle every attempt for economic betterment. If the workingman wants to avoid these
effects, he should *insist* on the right of the convict to
work, he should meet him as a brother, take him into
his organization, and *with his aid turn against the system which grinds them both.*

Last, but not least, is the growing realization of
the barbarity and the inadequacy of the definite sentence. Those who believe in, and earnestly aim at, a
change are fast coming to the conclusion that man
must be given an opportunity to make good. And
how is he to do it with ten, fifteen, or twenty years'
imprisonment before him? The hope of liberty and
of opportunity is the only incentive to life, especially
the prisoner's life. Society has sinned so long against

him—it ought at least to leave him that. I am not very sanguine that it will, or that any real change in that direction can take place until the conditions that breed both the prisoner and the jailer will be forever abolished.

> Out of his mouth a red, red rose!
> Out of his heart a white!
> For who can say by what strange way
> Christ brings his will to light,
> Since the barren staff the pilgrim bore
> Bloomed in the great Pope's sight.

PATRIOTISM

A MENACE TO LIBERTY

WHAT is patriotism? Is it love of one's birthplace, the place of childhood's recollections and hopes, dreams and aspirations? Is it the place where, in childlike naivety, we would watch the fleeting clouds, and wonder why we, too, could not run so swiftly? The place where we would count the milliard glittering stars, terror-stricken lest each one "an eye should be," piercing the very depths of our little souls? Is it the place where we would listen to the music of the birds, and long to have wings to fly, even as they, to distant lands? Or the place where we would sit at mother's knee, enraptured by wonderful tales of great deeds and conquests? In short, is it love for the spot, every inch representing dear and precious recollections of a happy, joyous, and playful childhood?

If that were patriotism, few American men of today could be called upon to be patriotic, since the place of play has been turned into factory, mill, and mine, while deafening sounds of machinery have replaced the music of the birds. Nor can we longer hear the tales of great deeds, for the stories our mothers tell today are but those of sorrow, tears, and grief.

What, then, is patriotism? "Patriotism, sir, is the last resort of scoundrels," said Dr. Johnson. Leo Tolstoy, the greatest anti-patriot of our times, defines patriotism as the principle that will justify the training of wholesale murderers; a trade that requires better equipment for the exercise of man-killing than the making of such necessities of life as shoes, clothing, and houses; a trade that guarantees better returns and greater glory than that of the average workingman.

Gustave Hervé, another great anti-patriot, justly calls patriotism a superstition—one far more injurious, brutal, and inhumane than religion. The superstition of religion originated in man's inability to explain natural phenomena. That is, when primitive man heard thunder or saw the lightning, he could not account for either, and therefore concluded that back of them must be a force greater than himself. Similarly he saw a supernatural force in the rain, and in the various other changes in nature. Patriotism, on the other hand, is a superstition artificially created and maintained through a network of lies and falsehoods; a superstition that robs man of his self-respect and dignity, and increases his arrogance and conceit.

Indeed, conceit, arrogance, and egotism are the essentials of patriotism. Let me illustrate. Patriotism assumes that our globe is divided into little spots, each one surrounded by an iron gate. Those who have had the fortune of being born on some particular spot, consider themselves better, nobler, grander, more intelligent than the living beings inhabiting any other spot. It is, therefore, the duty of everyone living on that chosen spot to fight, kill, and die in the attempt to impose his superiority upon all the others.

The inhabitants of the other spots reason in like manner, of course, with the result that, from early infancy, the mind of the child is poisoned with blood-curdling stories about the Germans, the French, the Italians, Russians, etc. When the child has reached manhood, he is thoroughly saturated with the belief that he is chosen by the Lord himself to defend *his* country against the attack or invasion of any foreigner. It is for that purpose that we are clamoring for a greater army and navy, more battleships and ammunition. It is for that purpose that America has within a short time spent four hundred million dollars. Just think of it—four hundred million dollars taken from the produce of *the people*. For surely it is not the rich who contribute to patriotism. They are cosmopolitans, perfectly at home in every land. We in America know well the truth of this. Are not our rich Americans Frenchmen in France, Germans in Germany, or Englishmen in England? And do they not squandor with cosmopolitan grace fortunes coined by American factory children and cotton slaves? Yes, theirs is the patriotism that will make it possible to send messages of condolence to a despot like the Russian Tsar, when any mishap befalls him, as President Roosevelt did in the name of *his* people, when Sergius was punished by the Russian revolutionists.

It is a patriotism that will assist the arch-murderer, Diaz, in destroying thousands of lives in Mexico, or that will even aid in arresting Mexican revolutionists on American soil and keep them incarcerated in

American prisons, without the slightest cause or reason.

But, then, patriotism is not for those who represent wealth and power. It is good enough for the people. It reminds one of the historic wisdom of Frederick the Great, the bosom friend of Voltaire, who said: "Religion is a fraud, but it must be maintained for the masses."

That patriotism is rather a costly institution, no one will doubt after considering the following statistics. The progressive increase of the expenditures for the leading armies and navies of the world during the last quarter of a century is a fact of such gravity as to startle every thoughtful student of economic problems. It may be briefly indicated by dividing the time from 1881 to 1905 into five-year periods, and noting the disbursements of several great nations for army and navy purposes during the first and last of those periods. From the first to the last of the periods noted the expenditures of Great Britain increased from $2,101,848,936 to $4,143,226,885, those of France from $3,324,500,000 to $3,455,109,900, those of Germany from $725,000,200 to $2,700,375,600, those of the United States from $1,275,500,750 to $2,650,900,450, those of Russia from $1,900,975,500 to $5,250,445,100, those of Italy from $1,600,975,750 to $1,755,500,100, and those of Japan from $182,900,500 to $700,925,475.

The military expenditures of each of the nations mentioned increased in each of the five-year periods under review. During the entire interval from 1881 to 1905 Great Britain's outlay for her army increased fourfold, that of the United States was tripled, Russia's was doubled, that of Germany increased 35 per cent., that of France about 15 per cent., and that of Japan nearly 500 per cent. If we compare the expenditures of these nations upon their armies with their total expenditures for all the twenty-five years ending with 1905, the proportion rose as follows:

In Great Britain from 20 per cent. to 37; in the United States from 15 to 23; in France from 16 to 18; in Italy from 12 to 15; in Japan from 12 to 14. On the other hand, it is interesting to note that the proportion in Germany decreased from about 58 per cent. to 25, the decrease being due to the enormous increase in the imperial expenditures for other purposes, the fact being that the army expenditures for the period of 1901-5 were higher than for any five-year period preceding. Statistics show that the countries in which army expenditures are greatest, in proportion to the total national revenues, are Great Britain, the United States, Japan, France, and Italy, in the order named.

The showing as to the cost of great navies is equally impressive. During the twenty-five years ending with 1905 naval expenditures increased approximately as follows: Great Britain, 300 per cent.; France 60 per cent.; Germany 600 per cent.; the United States 525 per cent.; Russia 300 per cent.; Italy 250 per cent.; and Japan, 700 per cent. With the exception of Great Britain, the United States spends more for naval purposes than any other nation, and this expenditure bears also a larger proportion to the entire national disbursements than that of any other power. In the period 1881-5, the expenditure for the United States navy was $6.20 out of each $100 appropriated for all national purposes; the amount rose to $6.60 for the next five-year period, to $8.10 for the next, to $11.70 for the next, and to $16.40 for 1901-5. It is morally certain that the outlay for the current period of five years will show a still further increase.

The rising cost of militarism may be still further illustrated by computing it as a per capita tax on population. From the first to the last of the five-year periods taken as the basis for the comparisons here given, it has risen as follows: In Great Britain, from $18.47 to $52.50; in France, from $19.66 to $23.62; in Germany, from $10.17 to $15.51; in the United States, from $5.62 to $13.64; in Russia, from $6.14 to $8.37; in Italy, from $9.59 to $11.24, and in Japan from 86 cents to $3.11.

It is in connection with this rough estimate of cost per capita that the economic burden of militarism is most appreciable. The irresistible conclusion from available data is that the increase of expenditure for army and navy purposes is rapidly surpassing the growth of population in each of the countries considered in the present calculation. In other words, a continuation of the increased demands of militarism threatens each of those nations with a progressive exhaustion both of men and resources.

The awful waste that patriotism necessitates ought to be sufficient to cure the man of even average intelligence from this disease. Yet patriotism demands still more. The people are urged to be patriotic and for that luxury they pay, not only by supporting their "defenders," but even by sacrificing their own children. Patriotism requires allegiance to the flag, which means obedience and readiness to kill father, mother, brother, sister.

The usual contention is that we need a standing army to protect the country from foreign invasion. Every intelligent man and woman knows, however, that this is a myth maintained to frighten and coerce the foolish. The governments of the world, knowing each other's interests, do not invade each other. They have learned that they can gain much more by international arbitration of disputes than by war and conquest. Indeed, as Carlyle said, "War is a quarrel between two thieves too cowardly to fight their own battle; therefore they take boys from one village and another village, stick them into uniforms, equip them with guns, and let them loose like wild beasts against each other."

It does not require much wisdom to trace every war back to a similar cause. Let us take our own Spanish-American war, supposedly a great and patriotic event in the history of the United States. How our hearts burned with indignation against the atrocious Spaniards! True, our indignation did not flare up spontaneously. It was nurtured by months of newspaper agitation, and long after Butcher Weyler had killed off many noble Cubans and outraged many Cuban women. Still, in justice to the American Nation be it said, it did grow indignant and was willing to fight, and that it fought bravely. But when the smoke was over, the dead buried, and the cost of the war came back to the people in an increase in the

price of commodities and rent—that is, when we
sobered up from our patriotic spree—it suddenly
dawned on us that the cause of the Spanish-American
war was the consideration of the price of sugar; or,
to be more explicit, that the lives, blood, and money
of the American people were used to protect the interests of American capitalists, which were threatened
by the Spanish government. That this is not an
exaggeration, but is based on absolute facts and
figures, is best proven by the attitude of the American
government to Cuban labor. When Cuba was firmly
in the clutches of the United States, the very soldiers
sent to liberate Cuba were ordered to shoot Cuban
workingmen during the great cigarmakers' strike,
which took place shortly after the war.

Nor do we stand alone in waging war for such
causes. The curtain is beginning to be lifted on the
motives of the terrible Russo-Japanese war, which
cost so much blood and tears. And we see again that
back of the fierce Moloch of war stands the still fiercer
god of Commercialism. Kuropatkin, the Russian
Minister of War during the Russo-Japanese struggle,
has revealed the true secret behind the latter. The
Tsar and his Grand Dukes, having invested money in
Corean concessions, the war was forced for the sole
purpose of speedily accumulating large fortunes.

The contention that a standing army and navy is
the best security of peace is about as logical as the
claim that the most peaceful citizen is he who goes
about heavily armed. The experience of every-day
life fully proves that the armed individual is invariably anxious to try his strength. The same is his-

torically true of governments. Really peaceful countries do not waste life and energy in war preparations, with the result that peace is maintained.

However, the clamor for an increased army and navy is not due to any foreign danger. It is owing to the dread of the growing discontent of the masses and of the international spirit among the workers. It is to meet the internal enemy that the Powers of various countries are preparing themselves; an enemy, who, once awakened to consciousness, will prove more dangerous than any foreign invader.

The powers that have for centuries been engaged in enslaving the masses have made a thorough study of their psychology. They know that the people at large are like children whose despair, sorrow, and tears can be turned into joy with a little toy. And the more gorgeously the toy is dressed, the louder the colors, the more it will appeal to the million-headed child.

An army and navy represents the people's toys. To make them more attractive and acceptable, hundreds and thousands of dollars are being spent for the display of these toys. That was the purpose of the American government in equipping a fleet and sending it along the Pacific coast, that every American citizen should be made to feel the pride and glory of the United States. The city of San Francisco spent one hundred thousand dollars for the entertainment of the fleet; Los Angeles, sixty thousand; Seattle and Tacoma, about one hundred thousand. To entertain the fleet, did I say? To dine and wine a few superior officers, while the "brave boys" had to mutiny to get sufficient food. Yes, two hundred and sixty thousand dollars were spent on fireworks, theatre parties, and revelries, at a time when men, women, and children through the breadth and length of the country were starving in the streets; when thousands of unemployed were ready to sell their labor at any price.

Two hundred and sixty thousand dollars! What could not have been accomplished with such an enormous sum? But instead of bread and shelter, the children of those cities were taken to see the fleet, that it may remain, as one of the newspapers said, "a lasting memory for the child."

A wonderful thing to remember, is it not? The implements of civilized slaughter. If the mind of the child is to be poisoned with such memories, what hope is there for a true realization of human brotherhood?

We Americans claim to be a peace-loving people. We hate bloodshed; we are opposed to violence. Yet we go into spasms of joy over the possibility of projecting dynamite bombs from flying machines upon helpless citizens. We are ready to hang, electrocute, or lynch anyone, who, from economic necessity, will risk his own life in the attempt upon that of some industrial magnate. Yet our hearts swell with pride at the thought that America is becoming the most powerful nation on earth, and that it will eventually plant her iron foot on the necks of all other nations.

Such is the logic of patriotism.

Considering the evil results that patriotism is fraught with for the average man, it is as nothing compared with the insult and injury that patriotism heaps upon the soldier himself,—that poor, deluded victim of superstition and ignorance. He, the savior of his country, the protector of his nation,—what has patriotism in store for him? A life of slavish submission, vice, and perversion, during peace; a life of danger, exposure, and death, during war.

While on a recent lecture tour in San Francisco, I visited the Presidio, the most beautiful spot overlooking the Bay and Golden Gate Park. Its purpose should have been playgrounds for children, gardens and music for the recreation of the weary. Instead it is made ugly, dull, and gray by barracks,—barracks wherein the rich would not allow their dogs to dwell. In these miserable shanties soldiers are herded like cattle; here they waste their young days, polishing the boots and brass buttons of their superior officers. Here, too, I saw the distinction of classes: sturdy sons of a free Republic, drawn up in line like convicts, saluting every passing shrimp of a lieutenant. American equality, degrading manhood and elevating the uniform!

Barrack life further tends to develop tendencies of sexual perversion. It is gradually producing along this line results similar to European military conditions. Havelock Ellis, the noted writer on sex psychology, has made a thorough study of the subject. I quote: "Some of the barracks are great centers of male prostitution. . . . The number of soldiers who prostitute themselves is greater than we are willing to believe. It is no exaggeration to say that in certain regiments the presumption is in favor of the venality of the majority of the men. . . . On summer even-ings Hyde Park and the neighborhood of Albert Gate are full of guardsmen and others plying a lively trade, and with little disguise, in uniform or out. . . . In most cases the proceeds form a comfortable addition to Tommy Atkins' pocket money."

To what extent this perversion has eaten its way into the army and navy can best be judged from the fact that special houses exist for this form of prostitution. The practice is not limited to England; it is universal. "Soldiers are no less sought after in France than in England or in Germany, and special houses for military prostitution exist both in Paris and the garrison towns."

Had Mr. Havelock Ellis included America in his investigation of sex perversion, he would have found that the same conditions prevail in our army and navy as in those of other countries. The growth of the standing army inevitably adds to the spread of sex perversion; the barracks are the incubators.

Aside from the sexual effects of barrack life, it also tends to unfit the soldier for useful labor after leaving the army. Men, skilled in a trade, seldom enter the army or navy, but even they, after a military experience, find themselves totally unfitted for their former occupations. Having acquired habits of idleness and a taste for excitement and adventure, no peaceful pursuit can content them. Released from the army, they can turn to no useful work. But it is usually the social riff-raff, discharged prisoners and the like, whom either the struggle for life or their own inclination drives into the ranks. These, their military term over, again turn to their former life of crime, more brutalized and degraded than before. It is a well-known fact that in our prisons there is a goodly number of ex-soldiers; while, on the other hand, the army and navy are to a great extent supplied with ex-convicts.

Of all the evil results I have just described none seems to me so detrimental to human integrity as the spirit patriotism has produced in the case of Private William Buwalda. Because he foolishly believed that one can be a soldier and exercise his rights as a man at the same time, the military authorities punished him severely. True, he had served his country fifteen years, during which time his record was unimpeachable. According to Gen. Funston, who reduced Buwalda's sentence to three years, "the first duty of an officer or an enlisted man is unquestioned obedience and loyalty to the government, and it makes no difference whether he approves of that government or not." Thus Funston stamps the true character of allegiance. According to him, entrance into the army abrogates the principles of the Declaration of Independence.

What a strange development of patriotism that turns a thinking being into a loyal machine!

In justification of this most outrageous sentence of Buwalda, Gen. Funston tells the American people that the soldier's action was "a serious crime equal to treason." Now, what did this "terrible crime" really consist of? Simply in this: William Buwalda was one of fifteen hundred people who attended a public meeting in San Francisco; and, oh, horrors, he shook hands with the speaker, Emma Goldman. A terrible crime, indeed, which the General calls "a great military offense, infinitely worse than desertion."

Can there be a greater indictment against patriotism than that it will thus brand a man a criminal, throw him into prison, and rob him of the results of fifteen years of faithful service?

Buwalda gave to his country the best years of his life and his very manhood. But all that was as nothing. Patriotism is inexorable and, like all insatiable monsters, demands all or nothing. It does not admit that a soldier is also a human being, who has a right to his own feelings and opinions, his own inclinations and ideas. No, patriotism can not admit of that. That is the lesson which Buwalda was made to learn; made to learn at a rather costly, though not at a useless price. When he returned to freedom, he had lost his position in the army, but he regained his self-respect. After all, that is worth three years of imprisonment.

A writer on the military conditions of America, in a recent article, commented on the power of the military man over the civilian in Germany. He said, among other things, that if our Republic had no other meaning than to guarantee all citizens equal rights, it would have just cause for existence. I am convinced that the writer was not in Colorado during the patriotic régime of General Bell. He probably would have changed his mind had he seen how, in the name of patriotism and the Republic, men were thrown into bull-pens, dragged about, driven across the border, and subjected to all kinds of indignities. Nor is that Colorado incident the only one in the growth of mili-

tary power in the United States. There is hardly a
strike where troops and militia do not come to the
rescue of those in power, and where they do not act as
arrogantly and brutally as do the men wearing the
Kaiser's uniform. Then, too, we have the Dick military law. Had the writer forgotten that?

A great misfortune with most of our writers is
that they are absolutely ignorant on current events, or
that, lacking honesty, they will not speak of these
matters. And so it has come to pass that the Dick
military law was rushed through Congress with little
discussion and still less publicity,—a law which gives
the President the power to turn a peaceful citizen into
a bloodthirsty man-killer, supposedly for the defense
of the country, in reality for the protection of the
interests of that particular party whose mouthpiece
the President happens to be.

Our writer claims that militarism can never
become such a power in America as abroad, since it is
voluntary with us, while compulsory in the Old World.
Two very important facts, however, the gentleman
forgets to consider. First, that conscription has
created in Europe a deep-seated hatred of militarism
among all classes of society. Thousands of young
recruits enlist under protest and, once in the army,
they will use every possible means to desert. Second,
that it is the compulsory feature of militarism which
has created a tremendous anti-militarist movement,
feared by European Powers far more than anything
else. After all, the greatest bulwark of capitalism is
militarism. The very moment the latter is undermined, capitalism will totter. True, we have no con-

scription; that is, men are not usually forced to enlist in the army, but we have developed a far more exacting and rigid force—necessity. Is it not a fact that during industrial depressions there is a tremendous increase in the number of enlistments? The trade of militarism may not be either lucrative or honorable, but it is better than tramping the country in search of work, standing in the bread line, or sleeping in municipal lodging houses. After all, it means thirteen dollars per month, three meals a day, and a place to sleep. Yet even necessity is not sufficiently strong a factor to bring into the army an element of character and manhood. No wonder our military authorities complain of the "poor material" enlisting in the army and navy. This admission is a very encouraging sign. It proves that there is still enough of the spirit of independence and love of liberty left in the average American to risk starvation rather than don the uniform.

Thinking men and women the world over are beginning to realize that patriotism is too narrow and limited a conception to meet the necessities of our time. The centralization of power has brought into being an international feeling of solidarity among the oppressed nations of the world; a solidarity which represents a greater harmony of interests between the workingman of America and his brothers abroad than between the American miner and his exploiting compatriot; a solidarity which fears not foreign invasion, because it is bringing all the workers to the point when they will say to their masters, "Go and do your own killing. We have done it long enough for you."

This solidarity is awakening the consciousness of

even the soldiers, they, too, being flesh of the flesh
of the great human family. A solidarity that has
proven infallible more than once during past struggles,
and which has been the impetus inducing the Parisian
soldiers, during the Commune of 1871, to refuse to
obey when ordered to shoot their brothers. It has
given courage to the men who mutinied on Russian
warships during recent years. It will eventually bring
about the uprising of all the oppressed and downtrodden against their international exploiters.

The proletariat of Europe has realized the great
force of that solidarity and has, as a result, inaugurated a war against patriotism and its bloody spectre,
militarism. Thousands of men fill the prisons of
France, Germany, Russia, and the Scandinavian
countries, because they dared to defy the ancient
superstition. Nor is the movement limited to the
working class; it has embraced representatives in all
stations of life, its chief exponents being men and
women prominent in art, science, and letters.

America will have to follow suit. The spirit of
militarism has already permeated all walks of life.
Indeed, I am convinced that militarism is growing a
greater danger here than anywhere else, because of
the many bribes capitalism holds out to those whom
it wishes to destroy.

The beginning has already been made in the
schools. Evidently the government holds to the
Jesuitical conception, "Give me the child mind, and
I will mould the man." Children are trained in military tactics, the glory of military achievements
extolled in the curriculum, and the youthful minds

perverted to suit the government. Further, the youth of the country is appealed to in glaring posters to join the army and navy. "A fine chance to see the world!" cries the governmental huckster. Thus innocent boys are morally shanghaied into patriotism, and the military Moloch strides conquering through the Nation.

The American workingman has suffered so much at the hands of the soldier, State and Federal, that he is quite justified in his disgust with, and his opposition to, the uniformed parasite. However, mere denunciation will not solve this great problem. What we need is a propaganda of education for the soldier: anti-patriotic literature that will enlighten him as to the real horrors of his trade, and that will awaken his consciousness to his true relation to the man to whose labor he owes his very existence.

It is precisely this that the authorities fear most. It is already high treason for a soldier to attend a radical meeting. No doubt they will also stamp it high treason for a soldier to read a radical pamphlet. But, then, has not authority from time immemorial stamped every step of progress as treasonable? Those, however, who earnestly strive for social reconstruction can well afford to face all that; for it is probably even more important to carry the truth into the barracks than into the factory. When we have undermined the patriotic lie, we shall have cleared the path for that great structure wherein all nationalities shall be united into a universal brotherhood,—a truly FREE SOCIETY.

FRANCISCO FERRER AND THE MODERN SCHOOL

EXPERIENCE has come to be considered the best school of life. The man or woman who does not learn some vital lesson in that school is looked upon as a dunce indeed. Yet strange to say, that though organized institutions continue perpetuating errors, though they learn nothing from experience, we acquiesce, as a matter of course.

There lived and worked in Barcelona a man by the name of Francisco Ferrer. A teacher of children he was, known and loved by his people. Outside of Spain only the cultured few knew of Francisco Ferrer's work. To the world at large this teacher was non-existent.

On the first of September, 1909, the Spanish government—at the behest of the Catholic Church—arrested Francisco Ferrer. On the thirteenth of October, after a mock trial, he was placed in the ditch at Montjuich prison, against the hideous wall of many sighs, and shot dead. Instantly Ferrer, the obscure teacher, became a universal figure, blazing forth the indignation and wrath of the whole civilized world against the wanton murder.

The killing of Francisco Ferrer was not the first crime committed by the Spanish government and the Catholic Church. The history of these institutions is one long stream of fire and blood. Still they have not learned through experience, nor yet come to realize that every frail being slain by Church and State grows and grows into a mighty giant, who will some day free humanity from their perilous hold.

Francisco Ferrer was born in 1859, of humble parents. They were Catholics, and therefore hoped to raise their son in the same faith. They did not know that the boy was to become the harbinger of a great truth, that his mind would refuse to travel in the old path. At an early age Ferrer began to question the faith of his fathers. He demanded to know how it is that the God who spoke to him of goodness and love would mar the sleep of the innocent child with dread and awe of tortures, of suffering, of hell. Alert and of a vivid and investigating mind, it did not take him long to discover the hideousness of that black monster, the Catholic Church. He would have none of it.

Francisco Ferrer was not only a doubter, a searcher for truth; he was also a rebel. His spirit would rise in just indignation against the iron régime of his country, and when a band of rebels, led by the brave patriot General Villacampa, under the banner of the Republican ideal, made an onslaught on that régime, none was more ardent a fighter than young Francisco Ferrer. The Republican ideal,—I hope no one will confound it with the Republicanism of this country. Whatever objection I, as an Anarchist, have to the Republicans of Latin countries, I know they tower high above that corrupt and reactionary party which, in America, is destroying every vestige of liberty and justice. One has but to think of the Mazzinis, the Garibaldis, the scores of others, to realize that their efforts were directed, not merely against the overthrow of despotism, but particularly against the Catholic Church, which from its very inception has been the enemy of all progress and liberalism.

In America it is just the reverse. Republicanism stands for vested rights, for imperialism, for graft, for the annihilation of every semblance of liberty. Its ideal is the oily, creepy respectability of a McKinley, and the brutal arrogance of a Roosevelt.

The Spanish republican rebels were subdued. It takes more than one brave effort to split the rock of ages, to cut off the head of that hydra monster, the Catholic Church and the Spanish throne. Arrest, persecution, and punishment followed the heroic attempt of the little band. Those who could escape the bloodhounds had to flee for safety to foreign shores. Francisco Ferrer was among the latter. He went to France.

How his soul must have expanded in the new land! France, the cradle of liberty, of ideas, of action. Paris, the ever young, intense Paris, with her pulsating life, after the gloom of his own belated country,—how she must have inspired him. What opportunities, what a glorious chance for a young idealist.

Francisco Ferrer lost no time. Like one famished

he threw himself into the various liberal movements, met all kinds of people, learned, absorbed, and grew. While there, he also saw in operation the Modern School, which was to play such an important and fatal part in his life.

The Modern School in France was founded long before Ferrer's time. Its originator, though on a small scale, was that sweet spirit Louise Michel. Whether consciously or unconsciously, our own great Louise felt long ago that the future belongs to the young generation; that unless the young be rescued from that mind and soul-destroying institution, the bourgeois school, social evils will continue to exist. Perhaps she thought, with Ibsen, that the atmosphere is saturated with ghosts, that the adult man and woman have so many superstitions to overcome. No sooner do they outgrow the deathlike grip of one spook, lo! they find themselves in the thraldom of ninety-nine other spooks. Thus but a few reach the mountain peak of complete regeneration.

The child, however, has no traditions to overcome. Its mind is not burdened with set ideas, its heart has not grown cold with class and caste distinctions. The child is to the teacher what clay is to the sculptor. Whether the world will receive a work of art or a wretched imitation, depends to a large extent on the creative power of the teacher.

Louise Michel was pre-eminently qualified to meet the child's soul cravings. Was she not herself of a childlike nature, so sweet and tender, unsophisticated and generous? The soul of Louise burned always at white heat over every social injustice. She was invariably in the front ranks whenever the people of Paris rebelled against some wrong. And as she was made to suffer imprisonment for her great devotion to the oppressed, the little school on Montmartre was soon no more. But the seed was planted and has since borne fruit in many cities of France.

The most important venture of a Modern School was that of the great young old man Paul Robin. Together with a few friends he established a large school at Cempuis, a beautiful place near Paris. Paul Robin aimed at a higher ideal than merely modern ideas in education. He wanted to demonstrate by actual facts that the burgeois conception of heredity is but a mere pretext to exempt society from its terrible crimes against the young. The contention that the child must suffer for the sins of the fathers, that it must continue in poverty and filth, that it must grow up a drunkard or criminal, just because its parents left it no other legacy, was too preposterous to the beautiful spirit of Paul Robin. He believed that whatever part heredity may play, there are other factors equally great, if not greater, that may and will eradicate or minimize the so-called first cause. Proper economic and social environment, the breath and freedom of nature, healthy exercise, love and sympathy, and, above all, a deep understanding for the needs of the child—these would destroy the cruel, unjust, and criminal stigma imposed on the innocent young.

Paul Robin did not select his children; he did not go to the so-called best parents: he took his material wherever he could find it. From the street, the hovels, the orphan and foundling asylums, the reformatories, from all those gray and hideous places where a benevolent society hides its victims in order to pacify its guilty conscience. He gathered all the dirty, filthy, shivering little waifs his place would hold, and brought them to Cempuis. There, surrounded by nature's own glory, free and unrestrained, well fed, clean kept, deeply loved and understood, the little human plants began to grow, to blossom, to develop beyond even the expectations of their friend and teacher, Paul Robin.

The children grew and developed into self-reliant, liberty-loving men and women. What greater danger to the institutions that make the poor in order to perpetuate the poor? Cempuis was closed by the French government on the charge of co-education, which is prohibited in France. However, Cempuis had been in operation long enough to prove to all advanced educators its tremendous possibilities, and to serve as an impetus for modern methods of education, that are slowly but inevitably undermining the present system.

Cempuis was followed by a great number of other educational attempts,—among them, by Madelaine Vernet, a gifted writer and poet, author of *l'Amour Libre,* and Sebastian Faure, with his *La Ruche,** which I visited while in Paris, in 1907.

Several years ago Comrade Faure bought the land on which he built his *La Ruche.* In a comparatively short time he succeeded in transforming the former

---

* *The Beehive.*

wild, uncultivated country into a blooming spot, having all the appearance of a well-kept farm. A large, square court, enclosed by three buildings, and a broad path leading to the garden and orchards, greet the eye of the visitor. The garden, kept as only a Frenchman knows how, furnishes a large variety of vegetables for *La Ruche*.

Sebastian Faure is of the opinion that if the child is subjected to contradictory influences, its development suffers in consequence. Only when the material needs, the hygiene of the home, and intellectual environment are harmonious, can the child grow into a healthy, free being.

Referring to his school, Sebastian Faure has this to say:

"I have taken twenty-four children of both sexes, mostly orphans, or those whose parents are too poor to pay. They are clothed, housed, and educated at my expense. Till their twelfth year they will receive a sound elementary education. Between the age of twelve and fifteen—their studies still continuing—they are to be taught some trade, in keeping with their individual disposition and abilities. After that they are at liberty to leave *La Ruche* to begin life in the outside world, with the assurance that they may at any time return to *La Ruche,* where they will be received with open arms and welcomed as parents do their beloved children. Then, if they wish to work at our place, they may do so under the following conditions: One third of the product to cover his or her expenses of maintenance, another third to go towards the general fund set aside for accommodating new children, and the last third to be devoted to the personal use of the child, as he or she may see fit.

"The health of the children who are now in my care is perfect. Pure air, nutritious food, physical exercise in the open, long walks, observation of hygienic rules, the short and interesting method of instruction, and, above all, our affectionate understanding and care of the children, have produced admirable physical and mental results.

"It would be unjust to claim that our pupils have accomplished wonders; yet, considering that they belong to the average, having had no previous opportunities, the results are very gratifying indeed. The most important thing they have acquired—a rare trait with ordinary school children—is the love of study, the desire to know, to be informed. They have learned a new method of work, one that quickens the memory and stimulates the imagination. We make a particular effort to awaken the child's interest in his surroundings, to make him realize the importance of observation, investigation, and reflection, so that when the children reach maturity, they would not be deaf and blind to the things about them. Our children never accept anything in blind faith, without inquiry as to why and wherefore; nor do they feel satisfied until their questions are thoroughly answered. Thus their minds are free from doubts and fear resultant from incomplete or untruthful replies; it is the latter which warp the growth of the child, and create a lack of confidence in himself and those about him.

"It is surprising how frank and kind and affectionate our little ones are to each other. The harmony between themselves and the adults at *La Ruche* is highly encouraging. We should feel at fault if the children were to fear or honor us merely because we are their elders. We leave nothing undone to gain their confidence and love; that accomplished, understanding will replace duty; confidence, fear; and affection, severity.

"No one has yet fully realized the wealth of sympathy, kindness, and generosity hidden in the soul of the child. The effort of every true educator should be to unlock that treasure—to stimulate the child's impulses, and call forth the best and noblest tendencies. What greater reward can there be for one whose life-work is to watch over the growth of the human plant, than to see its nature unfold its petals, and to observe it develop into a true individuality. My comrades at *La Ruche* look for no greater reward, and it is due to them and their efforts, even more than to my own, that our human garden promises to bear beautiful fruit."*

Regarding the subject of history and the prevailing old methods of instruction, Sebastian Faure said:

"We explain to our children that true history is yet to be written,—the story of those who have died, unknown, in the effort to aid humanity to greater achievement."†

Francisco Ferrer could not escape this great wave of Modern School attempts. He saw its possibilities, not merely in theoretic form, but in their practical application to every-day needs. He must have real-

* *Mother Earth*, 1907.
† *Ibid.*

ized that Spain, more than any other country, stands
in need of just such schools, if it is ever to throw
off the double yoke of priest and soldier.

When we consider that the entire system of education in Spain is in the hands of the Catholic Church,
and when we further remember the Catholic formula,
"To inculcate Catholicism in the mind of the child
until it is nine years of age is to ruin it forever for
any other idea," we will understand the tremendous
task of Ferrer in bringing the new light to his people.
Fate soon assisted him in realizing his great dream.

Mlle. Meunier, a pupil of Francisco Ferrer, and
a lady of wealth, became interested in the Modern
School project. When she died, she left Ferrer some
valuable property and twelve thousand francs yearly
income for the School.

It is said that mean souls can conceive of
naught but mean ideas. If so, the contemptible
methods of the Catholic Church to blackguard
Ferrer's character, in order to justify her own black
crime, can readily be explained. Thus the lie was
spread in American Catholic papers that Ferrer used
his intimacy with Mlle. Meunier to get possession of
her money.

Personally, I hold that the intimacy, of whatever nature, between a man and a woman, is their
own affair, their sacred own. I would therefore not
lose a word in referring to the matter, if it were
not one of the many dastardly lies circulated about
Ferrer. Of course, those who know the purity of
the Catholic clergy will understand the insinuation.
Have the Catholic priests ever looked upon woman

as anything but a sex commodity? The historical data regarding the discoveries in the cloisters and monasteries will bear me out in that. How, then, are they to understand the co-operation of a man and a woman, except on a sex basis?

As a matter of fact, Mlle. Meunier was considerably Ferrer's senior. Having spent her childhood and girlhood with a miserly father and a submissive mother, she could easily appreciate the necessity of love and joy in child life. She must have seen that Francisco Ferrer was a teacher, not college, machine, or diploma-made, but one endowed with genius for that calling.

Equipped with knowledge, with experience, and with the necessary means; above all, imbued with the divine fire of his mission, our Comrade came back to Spain, and there began his life's work. On the ninth of September, 1901, the first Modern School was opened. It was enthusiastically received by the people of Barcelona, who pledged their support. In a short address at the opening of the School, Ferrer submitted his program to his friends. He said: "I am not a speaker, not a propagandist, not a fighter. I am a teacher; I love children above everything. I think I understand them. I want my contribution to the cause of liberty to be a young generation ready to meet a new era."

He was cautioned by his friends to be careful in his opposition to the Catholic Church. They knew to what lengths she would go to dispose of an enemy. Ferrer, too, knew. But, like Brand, he believed in all or nothing. He would not erect the Modern School on the same old lie. He would be frank and honest and open with the children.

Francisco Ferrer became a marked man. From the very first day of the opening of the School, he was shadowed. The school building was watched, his little home in Mangat was watched. He was followed every step, even when he went to France or England to confer with his colleagues. He was a marked man, and it was only a question of time when the lurking enemy would tighten the noose.

It succeeded, almost, in 1906, when Ferrer was implicated in the attempt on the life of Alfonso. The evidence exonerating him was too strong even for the black crows;* they had to let him go—not for good, however. They waited. Oh, they can wait, when they have set themselves to trap a victim.

The moment came at last, during the anti-military uprising in Spain, in July, 1909. One will have to search in vain the annals of revolutionary history to find a more remarkable protest against militarism. Having been soldier-ridden for centuries, the people of Spain could stand the yoke no longer. They would refuse to participate in useless slaughter. They saw no reason for aiding a despotic government in subduing and oppressing a small people fighting for their independence, as did the brave Riffs. No, they would not bear arms against them.

For eighteen hundred years the Catholic Church has preached the gospel of peace. Yet, when the people actually wanted to make this gospel a living

* Black crows: The Catholic clergy.

reality, she urged the authorities to force them to bear arms. Thus the dynasty of Spain followed the murderous methods of the Russian dynasty,—the people were forced to the battlefield.

Then, and not until then, was their power of endurance at an end. Then, and not until then, did the workers of Spain turn against their masters, against those who, like leeches, had drained their strength, their very life-blood. Yes, they attacked the churches and the priests, but if the latter had a thousand lives, they could not possibly pay for the terrible outrages and crimes perpetrated upon the Spanish people.

Francisco Ferrer was arrested on the first of September, 1909. Until October first his friends and comrades did not even know what had become of him. On that day a letter was received by *L'Humanité* from which can be learned the whole mockery of the trial. And the next day his companion, Soledad Villafranca, received the following letter:

"No reason to worry; you know I am absolutely innocent. Today I am particularly hopeful and joyous. It is the first time I can write to you, and the first time since my arrest that I can bathe in the rays of the sun, streaming generously through my cell window. You, too, must be joyous."

How pathetic that Ferrer should have believed, as late as October fourth, that he would not be condemned to death. Even more pathetic that his friends and comrades should once more have made the blunder in crediting the enemy with a sense of justice. Time and again they had placed faith in the judicial powers, only to see their brothers killed before their very eyes. They made no preparation to rescue Ferrer, not even a protest of any extent; nothing. "Why, it is impossible to condemn Ferrer; he is innocent." But everything is possible with the Catholic Church. Is she not a practiced henchman, whose trials of her enemies are the worst mockery of justice?

On October fourth Ferrer sent the following letter to *L'Humanité:*

"The Prison Cell, Oct. 4, 1909.

"My dear Friends—Notwithstanding most absolute innocence, the prosecutor demands the death penalty, based on denunciations of the police, representing me as the chief of the world's Anarchists, directing the labor syndicates of France, and guilty of conspiracies and insurrections everywhere, and declaring that my voyages to London and Paris were undertaken with no other object.

"With such infamous lies they are trying to kill me.

"The messenger is about to depart and I have not time for more. All the evidence presented to the investigating judge by the police is nothing but a tissue of lies and calumnious insinuations. But no proofs against me, having done nothing at all.

"FERRER."

October thirteenth, 1909, Ferrer's heart, so brave, so staunch, so loyal, was stilled. Poor fools! The last agonized throb of that heart had barely died away when it began to beat a hundredfold in the hearts of the civilized world, until it grew into terrific thunder, hurling forth its malediction upon the instigators of the black crime. Murderers of black garb and pious mien, to the bar of justice!

Did Francisco Ferrer participate in the anti-military uprising? According to the first indictment, which appeared in a Catholic paper in Madrid, signed by the Bishop and all the prelates of Barcelona, he was not even accused of participation. The indictment was to the effect that Francisco Ferrer was guilty of having organized godless schools, and having circulated godless literature. But in the twentieth century men can not be burned merely for their godless beliefs. Something else had to be devised; hence the charge of instigating the uprising.

In no authentic source so far investigated could a single proof be found to connect Ferrer with the uprising. But then, no proofs were wanted, or accepted, by the authorities. There were seventy-two witnesses, to be sure, but their testimony was taken on paper. They never were confronted with Ferrer, or he with them.

Is it psychologically possible that Ferrer should have participated? I do not believe it is, and here are my reasons. Francisco Ferrer was not only a great teacher, but he was also undoubtedly a marvelous organizer. In eight years, between 1901-1909, he had organized in Spain one hundred and nine schools, besides inducing the liberal element of his country to organize three hundred and eight other schools.

In connection with his own school work, Ferrer had equipped a modern printing plant, organized a staff of translators, and spread broadcast one hundred and fifty thousand copies of modern scientific and so-ciologic works, not to forget the large quantity of rationalist text books. Surely none but the most methodical and efficient organizer could have accom-plished such a feat.

On the other hand, it was absolutely proven that the anti-military uprising was not at all organized; that it came as a surprise to the people them-selves, like a great many revolutionary waves on previous occasions. The people of Barcelona, for instance, had the city in their control for four days, and, according to the statement of tourists, greater order and peace never prevailed. Of course, the people were so little prepared that when the time came, they did not know what to do. In this regard they were like the people of Paris during the Com-mune of 1871. They, too, were unprepared. While they were starving, they protected the warehouses filled to the brim with provisions. They placed sen-tinels to guard the Bank of France, where the bour-geoisie kept the stolen money. The workers of Barcelona, too, watched over the spoils of their masters.

How pathetic is the stupidity of the underdog; how terribly tragic! But, then, have not his fetters been forged so deeply into his flesh, that he would not, even if he could, break them? The awe of authority, of law, of private property, hundredfold burned into his soul,—how is he to throw it off unprepared, unexpectedly?

Can anyone assume for a moment that a man like Ferrer would affiliate himself with such a spontaneous, unorganized effort? Would he not have known that it would result in a defeat, a disastrous defeat for the people? And is it not more likely that if he would have taken part, he, the experienced *entrepreneur*, would have thoroughly organized the attempt? If all other proofs were lacking, that one factor would be sufficient to exonerate Francisco Ferrer. But there are others equally convincing.

For the very date of the outbreak, July twenty-fifth, Ferrer had called a conference of his teachers and members of the League of Rational Education. It was to consider the autumn work, and particularly the publication of Elisée Reclus' great book, *L'Homme et la Terre,* and Peter Kropotkin's *Great French Revolution.* Is it at all likely, is it at all plausible that Ferrer, knowing of the uprising, being a party to it, would in cold blood invite his friends and colleagues to Barcelona for the day on which he realized their lives would be endangered? Surely, only the criminal, vicious mind of a Jesuit could credit such deliberate murder.

Francisco Ferrer had his life-work mapped out; he had everything to lose and nothing to gain, except ruin and disaster, were he to lend assistance to the outbreak. Not that he doubted the justice of the people's wrath; but his work, his hope, his very nature was directed toward another goal.

In vain are the frantic efforts of the Catholic

Church, her lies, falsehoods, calumnies. She stands condemned by the awakened human conscience of having once more repeated the foul crimes of the past.

Francisco Ferrer is accused of teaching the children the most blood-curdling ideas,—to hate God, for instance. Horrors! Francisco Ferrer did not believe in the existence of a God. Why teach the child to hate something which does not exist? Is it not more likely that he took the children out into the open, that he showed them the splendor of the sunset, the brilliancy of the starry heavens, the awe-inspiring wonder of the mountains and seas; that he explained to them in his simple, direct way the law of growth, of development, of the interrelation of all life? In so doing he made it forever impossible for the poisonous weeds of the Catholic Church to take root in the child's mind.

It has been stated that Ferrer prepared the children to destroy the rich. Ghost stories of old maids. Is it not more likely that he prepared them to succor the poor? That he taught them the humiliation, the degradation, the awfulness of poverty, which is a vice and not a virtue; that he taught the dignity and importance of all creative efforts, which alone sustain life and build character. Is it not the best and most effective way of bringing into the proper light the absolute uselessness and injury of parasitism?

Last, but not least, Ferrer is charged with undermining the army by inculcating anti-military ideas. Indeed? He must have believed with Tolstoy that war is legalized slaughter, that it perpetuates hatred and arrogance, that it eats away the heart of nations, and turns them into raving maniacs.

However, we have Ferrer's own word regarding his ideas of modern education:

"I would like to call the attention of my readers to this idea: All the value of education rests in the respect for the physical, intellectual, and moral will of the child. Just as in science no demonstration is possible save by facts, just so there is no real education save that which is exempt from all dogmatism, which leaves to the child itself the direction of its effort, and confines itself to the seconding of its effort. Now, there is nothing easier than to alter this purpose, and nothing harder than to respect it. Education is always imposing, violating, constraining; the real educator is he who can best protect the child against his (the teacher's) own ideas, his peculiar whims; he who can best appeal to the child's own energies.

"We are convinced that the education of the future will be of an entirely spontaneous nature; certainly we can not as yet realize it, but the evolution of methods in the direction of a wider comprehension of the phenomena of life, and the fact that all advances toward perfection mean the overcoming of restraint,—all this indicates that we are in the right when we hope for the deliverance of the child through science.

"Let us not fear to say that we want men capable of evolving without stopping, capable of destroying and renewing their environments without cessation, of renewing themselves also; men, whose intellectual independence will be their greatest force, who will attach themselves to nothing, always ready to accept what is best, happy in the triumph of new ideas, aspiring to live multiple lives in one life. Society fears such men; we therefore must not hope that it will ever want an education able to give them to us.

"We shall follow the labors of the scientists who study the child with the greatest attention, and we shall eagerly seek for means of applying their experience to the education which we want to build up, in the direction of an ever fuller liberation of the individual. But how can we attain our end? Shall it not be by putting ourselves directly to the work favoring the foundation of new schools, which shall be ruled as much as possible by this spirit of liberty, which we forefeel will dominate the entire work of education in the future?

"A trial has been made, which, for the present, has already given excellent results. We can destroy all which in the present school answers to the organization of constraint, the artificial surroundings by which children are separated from nature and life, the intellectual and moral discipline made use of to impose ready-made ideas upon them, beliefs which deprave and annihilate natural bent. Without fear of deceiving ourselves, we can restore the child to the environment which entices it, the environment of nature in which he will be in contact with all that he loves, and in which impressions of life will replace fastidious book-learning. If we did no more than that, we should already have prepared in great part the deliverance of the child.

"In such conditions we might already freely apply the data of science and labor most fruitfully.

"I know very well we could not thus realize all our hopes, that we should often be forced, for lack of knowledge, to employ undesirable methods; but a certitude would sustain us in our efforts—namely, that even without reaching our aim completely we should do more and better in our still imperfect work than the present school accomplishes. I like the free spontaneity of a child who knows nothing, better than the world-knowledge and intellectual deformity of a child who has been subjected to our present education."*

Had Ferrer actually organized the riots, had he fought on the barricades, had he hurled a hundred bombs, he could not have been so dangerous to the Catholic Church and to despotism, as with his opposition to discipline and restraint. Discipline and restraint—are they not back of all the evils in the world? Slavery, submission, poverty, all misery, all social iniquities result from discipline and restraint. Indeed, Ferrer was dangerous. Therefore he had to die, October thirteenth, 1909, in the ditch of Montjuich. Yet who dare say his death was in vain? In view of the tempestuous rise of universal indignation: Italy naming streets in memory of Francisco Ferrer, Belgium inaugurating a movement to erect a memorial; France calling to the front her most illustrious men to resume the heritage of the martyr; England being the first to issue a biography; all countries

---

* *Mother Earth*, December, 1909.

uniting in perpetuating the great work of Francisco
Ferrer; America, even, tardy always in progressive
ideas, giving birth to a Francisco Ferrer Association, its aim being to publish a complete life of Ferrer
and to organize Modern Schools all over the country,—in the face of this international revolutionary
wave, who is there to say Ferrer died in vain?

That death at Montjuich,—how wonderful, how
dramatic it was, how it stirs the human soul. Proud
and erect, the inner eye turned toward the light,
Francisco Ferrer needed no lying priests to give him
courage, nor did he upbraid a phantom for forsaking
him. The consciousness that his executioners represented a dying age, and that his was the living truth,
sustained him in the last heroic moments.

> A dying age and a living truth,
> The living burying the dead.

THE HYPOCRISY OF PURITANISM

SPEAKING of Puritanism in relation to American art, Mr. Gutzon Borglum said: "Puritanism has made us self-centered and hypocritical for so long, that sincerity and reverence for what is natural in our impulses have been fairly bred out of us, with the result that there can be neither truth nor individuality in our art."

Mr. Borglum might have added that Puritanism has made life itself impossible. More than art, more than estheticism, life represents beauty in a thousand variations; it is, indeed, a gigantic panorama of eternal change. Puritanism, on the other hand, rests on a fixed and immovable conception of life; it is based on the Calvinistic idea that life is a curse, imposed upon man by the wrath of God. In order to redeem himself man must do constant penance, must repudiate every natural and healthy impulse, and turn his back on joy and beauty.

Puritanism celebrated its reign of terror in England during the sixteenth and seventeenth centuries, destroying and crushing every manifestation of art and culture. It was the spirit of Puritanism which robbed Shelley of his children, because he would not bow to the dicta of religion. It was the same narrow spirit which alienated Byron from his native land, because that great genius rebelled against the monotony, dullness, and pettiness of his country. It was Puritanism, too, that forced some of England's freest women into the conventional lie of marriage: Mary Wollstonecraft and, later, George Eliot. And recently Puritanism has demanded another toll—the life of Oscar Wilde. In fact, Puritanism has never ceased to be the most pernicious factor in the domain of John Bull, acting as censor of the artistic expression of his people, and stamping its approval only on the dullness of middle-class respectability.

It is therefore sheer British jingoism which points to America as the country of Puritanic provincialism. It is quite true that our life is stunted by Puritanism, and that the latter is killing what is natural and healthy in our impulses. But it is equally true that it is to England that we are indebted for transplanting this spirit on American soil. It was bequeathed to us by the Pilgrim fathers. Fleeing from persecution and oppression, the Pilgrims of Mayflower fame established in the New World a reign of Puritanic tyranny and crime. The history of New England, and especially of Massachusetts, is full of the horrors that have turned life into gloom, joy and despair, naturalness into disease, honesty and truth into hideous lies and hypocrisies. The ducking-stool and whipping-post, as well as numerous other devices of torture, were the favorite English methods for American purification.

Boston, the city of culture, has gone down in the annals of Puritanism as the "Bloody Town." It rivaled Salem, even, in her cruel persecution of unauthorized religious opinions. On the now famous Common a half-naked woman, with a baby in her arms, was publicly whipped for the crime of free speech; and on the same spot Mary Dyer, another Quaker woman, was hanged in 1659. In fact, Boston has been the scene of more than one wanton crime committed by Puritanism. Salem, in the summer of 1692, killed eighteen people for witchcraft. Nor was Massachusetts alone in driving out the devil by fire and brimstone. As Canning justly said: "The Pilgrim fathers infested the New World to redress the balance of the Old." The horrors of that period have found their most supreme expression in the American classic, *The Scarlet Letter*.

Puritanism no longer employs the thumbscrew and lash; but it still has a most pernicious hold on the minds and feelings of the American people. Naught else can explain the power of a Comstock. Like the Torquemadas of ante-bellum days, Anthony Comstock is the autocrat of American morals; he dictates the standards of good and evil, of purity and vice. Like a thief in the night he sneaks into the private lives of the people, into their most intimate relations. The system of espionage established by this man Comstock puts to shame the infamous Third Division of the Russian secret police. Why does the public tolerate such an outrage on its liberties? Simply because Comstock is but the loud expression of the Puritanism bred in the Anglo-Saxon blood, and from whose thraldom even liberals have not succeeded in fully emancipating themselves. The visionless and leaden elements of the old Young Men's and Women's Christian Temperance Unions, Purity Leagues, American Sabbath Unions, and the Prohibition Party, with Anthony Comstock as their patron saint, are the grave diggers of American art and culture.

Europe can at least boast of a bold art and literature which delve deeply into the social and sexual problems of our time, exercising a severe critique of all our shams. As with a surgeon's knife every Puritanic carcass is dissected, and the way thus cleared for man's liberation from the dead weights of the past. But with Puritanism as the constant check upon American life, neither truth nor sincerity is possible. Nothing but gloom and mediocrity to dictate human conduct, curtail natural expression, and stifle our best impulses. Puritanism in this the twentieth century is as much the enemy of freedom and beauty as it was when it landed on Plymouth Rock. It repudiates, as something vile and sinful, our deepest feelings; but being absolutely ignorant as to the real functions of human emotions, Puritanism is itself the creator of the most unspeakable vices.

The entire history of asceticism proves this to be only too true. The Church, as well as Puritanism, has fought the flesh as something evil; it had to be subdued and hidden at all cost. The result of this vicious attitude is only now beginning to be recognized by modern thinkers and educators. They realize that "nakedness has a hygienic value as well as a spiritual significance, far beyond its influences in allaying the natural inquisitiveness of the young or acting as a preventative of morbid emotion. It is an inspiration to adults who have long outgrown any youthful curiosities. The vision of the essential and eternal human form, the nearest thing to us in all the world, with its vigor and its beauty and its grace, is one of the prime tonics of life."* But the spirit of purism has so perverted the human mind that it has lost the power to appreciate the beauty of nudity, forcing us to hide the natural form under the plea of chastity. Yet chastity itself is but an artificial imposition upon nature, expressive of a false shame of the human form. The modern idea of chastity, especially in reference to woman, its greatest victim, is but the sensuous exaggeration of our natural impulses. "Chastity varies with the amount of clothing," and hence Christians and purists forever hasten to cover the "heathen" with tatters, and thus convert him to goodness and chastity.

Puritanism, with its perversion of the significance and functions of the human body, especially in regard to woman, has condemned her to celibacy, or to the indiscriminate breeding of a diseased race, or to prostitution. The enormity of this crime against humanity is apparent when we consider the results. Absolute sexual continence is imposed upon the unmarried woman, under pain of being considered immoral or fallen, with the result of producing neurasthenia, impotence, depression, and a great variety of nervous

---

* *The Psychology of Sex.* Havelock Ellis.

complaints involving diminished power of work, limited enjoyment of life, sleeplessness, and preoccupation with sexual desires and imaginings. The arbitrary and pernicious dictum of total continence probably also explains the mental inequality of the sexes. Thus Freud believes that the intellectual inferiority of so many women is due to the inhibition of thought imposed upon them for the purpose of sexual repression. Having thus suppressed the natural sex desires of the unmarried woman, Puritanism, on the other hand, blesses her married sister for incontinent fruitfulness in wedlock. Indeed, not merely blesses her, but forces the woman, oversexed by previous repression, to bear children, irrespective of weakened physical condition or economic inability to rear a large family. Prevention, even by scientifically determined safe methods, is absolutely prohibited; nay, the very mention of the subject is considered criminal.

Thanks to this Puritanic tyranny, the majority of women soon find themselves at the ebb of their physical resources. Ill and worn, they are utterly unable to give their children even elementary care. That, added to economic pressure, forces many women to risk utmost danger rather than continue to bring forth life. The custom of procuring abortions has reached such vast proportions in America as to be almost beyond belief. According to recent investigations along this line, seventeen abortions are committed in every hundred pregnancies. This fearful percentage represents only cases which come to the knowledge of physicians. Considering the secrecy in which this practice is necessarily shrouded, and the consequent professional inefficiency and neglect, Puritanism continuously exacts thousands of victims to its own stupidity and hypocrisy.

Prostitution, although hounded, imprisoned, and chained, is nevertheless the greatest triumph of Puritanism. It is its most cherished child, all hypocritical sanctimoniousness notwithstanding. The prostitute is the fury of our century, sweeping across the "civilized" countries like a hurricane, and leaving a trail of disease and disaster. The only remedy Puritanism offers for this ill-begotten child is greater repression and more merciless persecution. The latest outrage is represented by the Page Law, which imposes upon the State of New York the terrible failure and crime of Europe, namely, registration and identification of the unfortunate victims of Puritanism. In equally stupid manner purism seeks to check the terrible scourge of its own creation—venereal diseases. Most disheartening it is that this spirit of obtuse narrow-mindedness has poisoned even our so-called liberals, and has blinded them into joining the crusade against the very things born of the hypocrisy of Puritanism—prostitution and its results. In wilful blindness Puritanism refuses to see that the true method of prevention is the one which makes it clear to all that "venereal diseases are not a mysterious or terrible thing, the penalty of the sin of the flesh, a sort of shameful evil branded by purist malediction, but an ordinary disease which may be treated and cured." By its methods of obscurity, disguise, and concealment, Puritanism has furnished favorable conditions for the growth

and spread of these diseases.   Its bigotry is again most
strikingly demonstrated by the senseless attitude in
regard to the great discovery of Prof. Ehrlich, hypocrisy veiling the important cure for syphilis with vague
allusions to a remedy for "a certain poison."

The almost limitless capacity of Puritanism for
evil is due to its intrenchment behind the State and
the law.   Pretending to safeguard the people against
"immorality," it has impregnated the machinery of
government and added to its usurpation of moral
guardianship the legal censorship of our views, feelings, and even of our conduct.

Art, literature, the drama, the privacy of the mails,
in fact, our most intimate tastes, are at the mercy of
this inexorable tyrant.   Anthony Comstock, or some
other equally ignorant policeman, has been given
power to desecrate genius, to soil and mutilate the
sublimest creation of nature—the human form.   Books
dealing with the most vital issues of our lives, and
seeking to shed light upon dangerously obscured
problems, are legaly treated as criminal offenses, and
their helpless authors thrown into prison or driven
to destruction and death.

Not even in the domain of the Tsar is personal liberty daily outraged to the extent it is in America, the
stronghold of the Puritanic eunuchs.   Here the only
day of recreation left to the masses, Sunday, has been
made hideous and utterly impossible.   All writers on
primitive customs and ancient civilization agree that
the Sabbath was a day of festivities, free from care
and duties, a day of general rejoicing and merry-
making.   In every European country this tradition

continues to bring some relief from the humdrum and stupidity of our Christian era. Everywhere concert halls, theaters, museums, and gardens are filled with men, women, and children, particularly workers with their families, full of life and joy, forgetful of the ordinary rules and conventions of their every-day existence. It is on that day that the masses demonstrate what life might really mean in a sane society, with work stripped of its profit-making, soul-destroying purpose.

Puritanism has robbed the people even of that one day. Naturally, only the workers are affected: our millionaires have their luxurious homes and elaborate clubs. The poor, however, are condemned to the monotony and dullness of the American Sunday. The sociability and fun of European outdoor life is here exchanged for the gloom of the church, the stuffy, germ-saturated country parlor, or the brutalizing atmosphere of the back-room saloon. In Prohibition States the people lack even the latter, unless they can invest their meager earnings in quantities of adulterated liquor. As to Prohibition, every one knows what a farce it really is. Like all other achievements of Puritanism it, too, has but driven the "devil" deeper into the human system. Nowhere else does one meet so many drunkards as in our Prohibition towns. But so long as one can use scented candy to abate the foul breath of hypocrisy, Puritanism is triumphant. Ostensibly Prohibition is opposed to liquor for reasons of health and economy, but the very spirit of Prohibition being itself abnormal, it succeeds but in creating an abnormal life.

Every stimulus which quickens the imagination and raises the spirits, is as necessary to our life as air. It invigorates the body, and deepens our vision of human fellowship. Without stimuli, in one form or another, creative work is impossible, nor indeed the spirit of kindliness and generosity. The fact that some great geniuses have seen their reflection in the goblet too frequently, does not justify Puritanism in attempting to fetter the whole gamut of human emotions. A Byron and a Poe have stirred humanity deeper than all the Puritans can ever hope to do. The former have given to life meaning and color; the latter are turning red blood into water, beauty into ugliness, variety into uniformity and decay. Puritanism, in whatever expression, is a poisonous germ. On the surface everything may look strong and vigorous; yet the poison works its way persistently, until the entire fabric is doomed. With Hippolyte Taine, every truly free spirit has come to realize that "Puritanism is the death of culture, philosophy, humor, and good fellowship; its characteristics are dullness, monotony, and gloom."

THE TRAFFIC IN WOMEN

OUR REFORMERS have suddenly made a great discovery—the white slave traffic. The papers are full of these "unheard-of conditions," and lawmakers are already planning a new set of laws to check the horror.

It is significant that whenever the public mind is to be diverted from a great social wrong, a crusade is inaugurated against indecency, gambling, saloons, etc. And what is the result of such crusades? Gambling is increasing, saloons are doing a lively business through back entrances, prostitution is at its height, and the system of pimps and cadets is but aggravated.

How is it that an institution, known almost to every child, should have been discovered so suddenly? How is it that this evil, known to all sociologists, should now be made such an important issue?

To assume that the recent investigation of the white slave traffic (and, by the way, a very superficial investigation) has discovered anything new, is, to say the least, very foolish. Prostitution has been, and is, a widespread evil, yet mankind goes on its business, perfectly indifferent to the sufferings and distress of the victims of prostitution. As indifferent, indeed, as mankind has remained to our industrial system, or to economic prostitution.

Only when human sorrows are turned into a toy with glaring colors will baby people become interested —for a while at least. The people are a very fickle baby that must have new toys every day. The "righteous" cry against the white slave traffic is such a toy. It serves to amuse the people for a little while, and it will help to create a few more fat political jobs—parasites who stalk about the world as inspectors, investigators, detectives, and so forth.

What is really the cause of the trade in women? Not merely white women, but yellow and black women as well. Exploitation, of course; the merciless Moloch of capitalism that fattens on underpaid labor, thus driving thousands of women and girls into prostitution. With Mrs. Warren these girls feel, "Why waste your life working for a few shillings a week in a scullery, eighteen hours a day?"

Naturally our reformers say nothing about this cause. They know it well enough, but it doesn't pay to say anything about it. It is much more profitable to play the Pharisee, to pretend an outraged morality, than to go to the bottom of things.

However, there is one commendable exception among the young writers: Reginald Wright Kauffman, whose work *The House of Bondage* is the first earnest attempt to treat the social evil—not from a sentimental Philistine viewpoint. A journalist of wide experience, Mr. Kauffman proves that our industrial system leaves most women no alternative except prostitution. The women portrayed in *The House of Bondage* belong to the working class. Had the author portrayed the life of women in other spheres, he would have been confronted with the same state of affairs.

Nowhere is woman treated according to the merit of her work, but rather as a sex. It is therefore almost inevitable that she should pay for her right to exist, to keep a position in whatever line, with sex favors. Thus it is merely a question of degree whether she sells herself to one man, in or out of marriage, or to many men. Whether our reformers admit it or not, the economic and social inferiority of woman is responsible for prostitution.

Just at present our good people are shocked by the disclosures that in New York City alone one out of every ten women works in a factory, that the average wage received by women is six dollars per week for forty-eight to sixty hours of work, and that the majority of female wage workers face many months of idleness which leaves the average wage about $280 a year. In view of these economic horrors, is it to be wondered at that prostitution and the white slave trade have become such dominant factors?

Lest the preceding figures be considered an exaggeration, it is well to examine what some authorities on prostitution have to say:

"A prolific cause of female depravity can be found in the several tables, showing the description of the employment pursued, and the wages received, by the women previous to their fall, and it will be a question for the political economist to decide how far mere business consideration should be an apology on the part of employers for a reduction in their rates of remuneration, and whether the savings of a small percentage on wages is not more than counterbalanced by the enormous amount of taxation enforced on the public at large to defray the expenses incurred on account of a system of vice, *which is the direct result, in many cases, of insufficient compensation of honest labor."*

Our present-day reformers would do well to look into Dr. Sanger's book. There they will find that out of 2,000 cases under his observation, but few came from the middle classes, from well-ordered conditions, or pleasant homes. By far the largest majority were working girls and working women; some driven into prostitution through sheer want, others because of a cruel, wretched life at home, others again because of thwarted and crippled physical natures (of which I shall speak later on). Also it will do the maintainers of purity and morality good to learn that out of two thousand cases, 490 were married women, women who lived with their husbands. Evidently there was not much of a guaranty for their "safety and purity" in the sanctity of marriage.†

---

*Dr. Sanger, *The History of Prostitution.*

† It is a significant fact that Dr. Sanger's book has been excluded from the U. S. mails. Evidently the authorities are not anxious that the public be informed as to the true cause of prostitution.

Dr. Alfred Blaschko, in *Prostitution in the Nine-teenth Century,* is even more emphatic in characteriz-ing economic conditions as one of the most vital factors of prostitution.

"Although prostitution has existed in all ages, it was left to the nineteenth century to develop it into a gigantic social institution. The development of in-dustry with vast masses of people in the competitive market, the growth and congestion of large cities, the insecurity and uncertainty of employment, has given prostitution an impetus never dreamed of at any period in human history."

And again Havelock Ellis, while not so absolute in dealing with the economic cause, is nevertheless compelled to admit that it is indirectly and directly the main cause. Thus he finds that a large percentage of prostitutes is recruited from the servant class, although the latter have less care and greater security. On the other hand, Mr. Ellis does not deny that the daily routine, the drudgery, the monotony of the servant girl's lot, and especially the fact that she may never partake of the companionship and joy of a home, is no mean factor in forcing her to seek recreation and forgetfulness in the gaiety and glim-mer of prostitution. In other words, the servant girl, being treated as a drudge, never having the right to herself, and worn out by the caprices of her mistress, can find an outlet, like the factory or shopgirl, only in prostitution.

The most amusing side of the question now be-fore the public is the indignation of our "good, respectable people," especially the various Christian gentlemen, who are always to be found in the front ranks of every crusade. Is it that they are absolutely ignorant of the history of religion, and especially of the Christian religion? Or is it that they hope to blind the present generation to the part played in the past by the Church in relation to prostitution? Whatever their reason, they should be the last to cry out against the unfortunate victims of today, since it is known to every intelligent student that prostitution is of religious origin, maintained and fostered for many centuries, not as a shame, but as a virtue, hailed as such by the Gods themselves.

"It would seem that the origin of prostitution is to be found primarily in a religious custom, religion, the great conserver of social tradition, preserving in a transformed shape a primitive freedom that was passing out of the general social life. The typical example is that recorded by Herodotus, in the fifth century before Christ, at the Temple of Mylitta, the Babylonian Venus, where every woman, once in her life, had to come and give herself to the first stranger, who threw a coin in her lap, to worship the goddess. Very similar customs existed in other parts of western Asia, in North Africa, in Cyprus, and other islands of the eastern Mediterranean, and also in Greece, where the temple of Aphrodite on the fort at Corinth possessed over a thousand hierodules, dedicated to the service of the goddess.

"The theory that religious prostitution developed, as a general rule, out of the belief that the generative activity of human beings possessed a mysterious and sacred influence in promoting the fertility of Nature, is maintained by all authoritative writers on the subject. Gradually, however, and when prostitution became an organized institution under priestly influence, religious prostitution developed utilitarian sides, thus helping to increase public revenue.

"The rise of Christianity to political power produced little change in policy. The leading fathers of the Church tolerated prostitution. Brothels under municipal protection are found in the thirteenth century. They constituted a sort of public service, the directors of them being considered almost as public servants."*

To this must be added the following from Dr. Sanger's work:

"Pope Clement II. issued a bull that prostitutes would be tolerated if they pay a certain amount of their earnings to the Church.

"Pope Sixtus IV. was more practical; from one single brothel, which he himself had built, he received an income of 20,000 ducats."

In modern times the Church is a little more careful in that direction. At least she does not openly demand tribute from prostitutes. She finds it much more profitable to go in for real estate, like Trinity Church, for instance, to rent out death traps at an exorbitant price to those who live off and by prostitution.

Much as I should like to, my space will not admit speaking of prostitution in Egypt, Greece, Rome, and during the Middle Ages. The conditions in the latter period are particularly interesting, inasmuch as pros-

---

*Havelock Ellis, *Sex and Society*.

titution was organized into guilds, presided over by a brothel queen. These guilds employed strikes as a medium of improving their condition and keeping a standard price. Certainly that is more practical a method than the one used by the modern wage-slave in society.

It would be one-sided and extremely superficial to maintain that the economic factor is the only cause of prostitution. There are others no less important and vital. That, too, our reformers know, but dare discuss even less than the institution that saps the very life out of both men and women. I refer to the sex question, the very mention of which causes most people moral spasms.

It is a conceded fact that woman is being reared as a sex commodity, and yet she is kept in absolute ignorance of the meaning and importance of sex. Everything dealing with that subject is suppressed, and persons who attempt to bring light into this terrible darkness are persecuted and thrown into prison. Yet it is nevertheless true that so long as a girl is not to know how to take care of herself, not to know the function of the most important part of her life, we need not be surprised if she becomes an easy prey to prostitution, or to any other form of a relationship which degrades her to the position of an object for mere sex gratification.

It is due to this ignorance that the entire life and nature of the girl is thwarted and crippled. We have long ago taken it as a self-evident fact that the boy may follow the call of the wild; that is to say, that the boy may, as soon as his sex nature asserts itself, satisfy that nature; but our moralists are scandalized at the very thought that the nature of a girl should assert itself. To the moralist prostitution does not consist so much in the fact that the woman sells her body, but rather that she sells it out of wedlock. That this is no mere statement is proved by the fact that marriage for monetary considerations is perfectly legitimate, sanctified by law and public opinion, while any other union is condemned and repudiated. Yet a prostitute, if properly defined, means nothing else than "any person for whom sexual relationships are subordinated to gain."*

"Those women are prostitutes who sell their bodies for the exercise of the sexual act and make of this a profession."†

In fact, Banger goes further; he maintains that the act of prostitution is "intrinsically equal to that of a man or woman who contracts a marriage for economic reasons."

Of course, marriage is the goal of every girl, but as thousands of girls cannot marry, our stupid social customs condemn them either to a life of celibacy or prostitution. Human nature asserts itself regardless of all laws, nor is there any plausible reason why nature should adapt itself to a perverted conception of morality.

Society considers the sex experiences of a man as attributes of his general development, while similar experiences in the life of a woman are looked upon as a terrible calamity, a loss of honor and of all that is

* Guyot, *La Prostitution.*
† Banger, *Criminalité et Condition Economique.*

good and noble in a human being. This double standard of morality has played no little part in the creation and perpetuation of prostitution. It involves the
keeping of the young in absolute ignorance on sex
matters, which alleged "innocence," together with an
overwrought and stifled sex nature, helps to bring
about a state of affairs that our Puritans are so
anxious to avoid or prevent.

Not that the gratification of sex must needs lead
to prostitution; it is the cruel, heartless, criminal persecution of those who dare divert from the beaten
track, which is responsible for it.

Girls, mere children, work in crowded, over-
heated rooms ten to twelve hours daily at a machine,
which tends to keep them in a constant over-excited
sex state. Many of these girls have no home or comforts of any kind; therefore the street or some place
of cheap amusement is the only means of forgetting
their daily routine. This naturally brings them into
close proximity with the other sex. It is hard to say
which of the two factors brings the girl's over-sexed
condition to a climax, but it is certainly the most
natural thing that a climax should result. That is the
first step toward prostitution. Nor is the girl to be
held responsible for it. On the contrary, it is altogether the fault of society, the fault of our lack of
understanding, of our lack of appreciation of life in
the making; especially is it the criminal fault of our
moralists, who condemn a girl for all eternity, because
she has gone from the "path of virtue"; that is,
because her first sex experience has taken place without the sanction of the Church.

The girl feels herself a complete outcast, with the doors of home and society closed in her face. Her entire training and tradition is such that the girl herself feels depraved and fallen, and therefore has no ground to stand upon, or any hold that will lift her up, instead of dragging her down. Thus society creates the victims that it afterwards vainly attempts to get rid of. The meanest, most depraved and decrepit man still considers himself too good to take as his wife the woman whose grace he was quite willing to buy, even though he might thereby save her from a life of horror. Nor can she turn to her own sister for help. In her stupidity the latter deems herself too pure and chaste, not realizing that her own position is in many respects even more deplorable than her sister's of the street.

"The wife who married for money, compared with the prostitute," says Havelock Ellis, "is the true scab. She is paid less, gives much more in return in labor and care, and is absolutely bound to her master. The prostitute never signs away the right over her own person, she retains her freedom and personal rights, nor is she always compelled to submit to man's embrace."

Nor does the better-than-thou woman realize the apologist claim of Lecky that "though she may be the supreme type of vice, she is also the most efficient guardian of virtue. But for her, happy homes would be polluted, unnatural and harmful practice would abound."

Moralists are ever ready to sacrifice one-half of the human race for the sake of some miserable

institution which they can not outgrow. As a matter
of fact, prostitution is no more a safeguard for the
purity of the home than rigid laws are a safeguard
against prostitution. Fully fifty per cent. of married
men are patrons of brothels. It is through this vir-
tuous element that the married women—nay, even
the children—are infected with venereal diseases.
Yet society has not a word of condemnation for the
man, while no law is too monstrous to be set in motion
against the helpless victim. She is not only preyed
upon by those who use her, but she is also absolutely
at the mercy of every policeman and miserable detective on the beat, the officials at the station house, the
authorities in every prison.

In a recent book by a woman who was for twelve
years the mistress of a "house," are to be found the
following figures: "The authorities compelled me to
pay every month fines between $14.70 to $29.70, the
girls would pay from $5.70 to $9.70 to the police."
Considering that the writer did her business in a small
city, that the amounts she gives do not include extra
bribes and fines, one can readily see the tremendous
revenue the police department derives from the blood
money of its victims, whom it will not even protect.
Woe to those who refuse to pay their toll; they would
be rounded up like cattle, "if only to make a favorable
impression upon the good citizens of the city, or if the
powers needed extra money on the side. For the
warped mind who believes that a fallen woman is
incapable of human emotion it would be impossible to
realize the grief, the disgrace, the tears, the wounded
pride that was ours every time we were pulled in."

Strange, isn't it, that a woman who has kept a "house" should be able to feel that way? But stranger still that a good Christian world should bleed and fleece such women, and give them nothing in return except obloquy and persecution. Oh, for the charity of a Christian world!

Much stress is laid on white slaves being imported into America. How would America ever retain her virtue if Europe did not help her out? I will not deny that this may be the case in some instances, any more than I will deny that there are emissaries of Germany and other countries luring economic slaves into America; but I absolutely deny that prostitution is recruited to any appreciable extent from Europe. It may be true that the majority of prostitutes of New York City are foreigners, but that is because the majority of the population is foreign. The moment we go to any other American city, to Chicago or the Middle West, we shall find that the number of foreign prostitutes is by far a minority.

Equally exaggerated is the belief that the majority of street girls in this city were engaged in this business before they came to America. Most of the girls speak excellent English, are Americanized in habits and appearance,—a thing absolutely impossible unless they had lived in this country many years. That is, they were driven into prostitution by American conditions, by the thoroughly American custom for excessive display of finery and clothes, which, of course, necessitates money,—money that cannot be earned in shops or factories.

In other words, there is no reason to believe that

any set of men would go to the risk and expense of getting foreign products, when American conditions are overflooding the market with thousands of girls. On the other hand, there is sufficient evidence to prove that the export of American girls for the purpose of prostitution is by no means a small factor.

Thus Clifford G. Roe, ex-Assistant State Attorney of Cook County, Ill., makes the open charge that New England girls are shipped to Panama for the express use of men in the employ of Uncle Sam. Mr. Roe adds that "there seems to be an underground railroad between Boston and Washington which many girls travel." Is it not significant that the railroad should lead to the very seat of Federal authority? That Mr. Roe said more than was desired in certain quarters is proved by the fact that he lost his position. It is not practical for men in office to tell tales from school.

The excuse given for the conditions in Panama is that there are no brothels in the Canal Zone. That is the usual avenue of escape for a hypocritical world that dares not face the truth. Not in the Canal Zone, not in the city limits,—therefore prostitution does not exist.

Next to Mr. Roe, there is James Bronson Reynolds, who has made a thorough study of the white slave traffic in Asia. As a staunch American citizen and friend of the future Napoleon of America, Theodore Roosevelt, he is surely the last to discredit the virtue of his country. Yet we are informed by him that in Hong Kong, Shanghai, and Yokohama, the Augean stables of American vice are located. There American prostitutes have made themselves so con-

spicuous that in the Orient "American girl" is synonymous with prostitute. Mr. Reynolds reminds his
countrymen that while Americans in China are under
the protection of our consular representatives, the
Chinese in America have no protection at all. Every
one who knows the brutal and barbarous persecution
Chinese and Japanese endure on the Pacific Coast,
will agree with Mr. Reynolds.

In view of the above facts it is rather absurd to
point to Europe as the swamp whence come all the
social diseases of America. Just as absurd is it to
proclaim the myth that the Jews furnish the largest
contingent of willing prey. I am sure that no one
will accuse me of nationalistic tendencies. I am glad
to say that I have developed out of them, as out of
many other prejudices. If, therefore, I resent the
statement that Jewish prostitutes are imported, it is
not because of any Judaistic sympathies, but because
of the facts inherent in the lives of these people. No
one but the most superficial will claim that Jewish
girls migrate to strange lands, unless they have some
tie or relation that brings them there. The Jewish
girl is not adventurous. Until recent years she had
never left home, not even so far as the next village or
town, except it were to visit some relative. Is it then
credible that Jewish girls would leave their parents or
families, travel thousands of miles to strange lands,
through the influence and promises of strange forces?
Go to any of the large incoming steamers and see for
yourself if these girls do not come either with their
parents, brothers, aunts, or other kinsfolk. There
may be exceptions, of course, but to state that large

numbers of Jewish girls are imported for prostitution, or any other purpose, is simply not to know Jewish psychology.

Those who sit in a glass house do wrong to throw stones about them; besides, the American glass house is rather thin, it will break easily, and the interior is anything but a gainly sight.

To ascribe the increase of prostitution to alleged importation, to the growth of the cadet system, or similar causes, is highly superficial. I have already referred to the former. As to the cadet system, abhorrent as it is, we must not ignore the fact that it is essentially a phase of modern prostitution,—a phase accentuated by suppression and graft, resulting from sporadic crusades against the social evil.

The procurer is no doubt a poor specimen of the human family, but in what manner is he more despicable than the policeman who takes the last cent from the street walker, and then locks her up in the station house? Why is the cadet more criminal, or a greater menace to society, than the owners of department stores and factories, who grow fat on the sweat of their victims, only to drive them to the streets? I make no plea for the cadet, but I fail to see why he should be mercilessly hounded, while the real perpetrators of all social iniquity enjoy immunity and respect. Then, too, it is well to remember that it is not the cadet who makes the prostitute. It is our sham and hypocrisy that create both the prostitute and the cadet.

Until 1894 very little was known in America of the procurer. Then we were attacked by an epidemic

of virtue. Vice was to be abolished, the country purified at all cost. The social cancer was therefore
driven out of sight, but deeper into the body. Keepers of brothels, as well as their unfortunate victims,
were turned over to the tender mercies of the police.
The inevitable consequence of exorbitant bribes, and
the penitentiary, followed.

While comparatively protected in the brothels,
where they represented a certain monetary value, the
girls now found themselves on the street, absolutely
at the mercy of the graft-greedy police. Desperate,
needing protection and longing for affection, these
girls naturally proved an easy prey for cadets, themselves the result of the spirit of our commercial age.
Thus the cadet system was the direct outgrowth of
police persecution, graft, and attempted suppression
of prostitution. It were sheer folly to confound this
modern phase of the social evil with the causes of the
latter.

Mere suppression and barbaric enactments can
serve but to embitter, and further degrade, the unfortunate victims of ignorance and stupidity. The latter
has reached its highest expression in the proposed law
to make humane treatment of prostitutes a crime,
punishing any one sheltering a prostitute with five
years' imprisonment and $10,000 fine. Such an atti-
tude merely exposes the terrible lack of understanding
of the true causes of prostitution, as a social factor,
as well as manifesting the Puritanic spirit of the
Scarlet Letter days.

There is not a single modern writer on the subject
who does not refer to the utter futility of legislative

methods in coping with the issue. Thus Dr. Blaschko finds that governmental suppression and moral crusades accomplish nothing save driving the evil into secret channels, multiplying its dangers to society. Havelock Ellis, the most thorough and humane student of prostitution, proves by a wealth of data that the more stringent the methods of persecution the worse the condition becomes. Among other data we learn that in France, "in 1560, Charles IX. abolished brothels through an edict, but the numbers of prostitutes were only increased, while many new brothels appeared in unsuspected shapes, and were more dangerous. In spite of all such legislation, *or because of it,* there has been no country in which prostitution has played a more conspicuous part."*

An educated public opinion, freed from the legal and moral hounding of the prostitute, can alone help to ameliorate present conditions. Wilful shutting of eyes and ignoring of the evil as a social factor of modern life, can but aggravate matters. We must rise above our foolish notions of "better than thou," and learn to recognize in the prostitute a product of social conditions. Such a realization will sweep away the attitude of hypocrisy, and insure a greater understanding and more humane treatment. As to a thorough eradication of prostitution, nothing can accomplish that save a complete transvaluation of all accepted values—especially the moral ones—coupled with the abolition of industrial slavery.

---

* *Sex and Society.*

WOMAN SUFFRAGE

WE BOAST of the age of advancement, of science, and progress. Is it not strange, then, that we still believe in fetich worship? True, our fetiches have different form and substance, yet in their power over the human mind they are still as disastrous as were those of old.

Our modern fetich is universal suffrage. Those who have not yet achieved that goal fight bloody revolutions to obtain it, and those who have enjoyed its reign bring heavy sacrifice to the altar of this omnipotent diety. Woe to the heretic who dare question that divinity!

Woman, even more than man, is a fetich worshipper, and though her idols may change, she is ever on her knees, ever holding up her hands, ever blind to the fact that her god has feet of clay. Thus woman has been the greatest supporter of all deities from time immemorial. Thus, too, she has had to pay the price that only gods can exact,—her freedom, her heart's blood, her very life.

Nietzsche's memorable maxim, "When you go to woman, take the whip along," is considered very brutal, yet Nietzsche expressed in one sentence the attitude of woman towards her gods.

Religion, especially the Christian religion, has condemned woman to the life of an inferior, a slave. It has thwarted her nature and fettered her soul, yet the Christian religion has no greater supporter, none more devout, than woman. Indeed, it is safe to say that religion would have long ceased to be a factor in the lives of the people, if it were not for the support it receives from woman. The most ardent churchworkers, the most tireless missionaries the world over, are women, always sacrificing on the altar of the gods that have chained her spirit and enslaved her body.

The insatiable monster, war, robs woman of all that is dear and precious to her. It exacts her brothers, lovers, sons, and in return gives her a life of loneliness and despair. Yet the greatest supporter and worshiper of war is woman. She it is who instills the love of conquest and power into her children; she it is who whispers the glories of war into the ears of her little ones, and who rocks her baby to sleep with the tunes of trumpets and the noise of guns. It is woman, too, who crowns the victor on his return from the battlefield. Yes, it is woman who pays the highest price to that insatiable monster, war.

Then there is the home. What a terrible fetich it is! How it saps the very life-energy of woman,— this modern prison with golden bars. Its shining aspect blinds woman to the price she would have to pay as wife, mother, and housekeeper. Yet woman clings tenaciously to the home, to the power that holds her in bondage.

It may be said that because woman recognizes the awful toll she is made to pay to the Church, State, and the home, she wants suffrage to set herself free. That may be true of the few; the majority of suffragists repudiate utterly such blasphemy. On the contrary, they insist always that it is woman suffrage which will make her a better Christian and home-keeper, a staunch citizen of the State. Thus suffrage is only a means of strengthening the omnipotence of the very Gods that woman has served from time immemorial.

What wonder, then, that she should be just as devout, just as zealous, just as prostrate before the new idol, woman suffrage. As of old, she endures persecution, imprisonment, torture, and all forms of condemnation, with a smile on her face. As of old, the most enlightened, even, hope for a miracle from the twentieth-century deity,—suffrage. Life, happiness, joy, freedom, independence,—all that, and more, is to spring from suffrage. In her blind devotion woman does not see what people of intellect perceived fifty years ago: that suffrage is an evil, that it has only helped to enslave people, that it has but closed their eyes that they may not see how craftily they were made to submit.

Woman's demand for equal suffrage is based largely on the contention that woman must have the equal right in all affairs of society. No one could, possibly, refute that, if suffrage were a right. Alas, for the ignorance of the human mind, which can see

a right in an imposition.   Or is it not the most brutal
imposition for one set of people to make laws that
another set is coerced by force to obey?   Yet woman
clamors for that "golden opportunity" that has
wrought so much misery in the world, and robbed
man of his integrity and self-reliance; an imposition
which has thoroughly corrupted the people, and made
them absolute prey in the hands of unscrupulous politicians.

The poor, stupid, free American citizen!   Free to
starve, free to tramp the highways of this great country, he enjoys universal suffrage, and, by that right,
he has forged chains about his limbs.   The reward
that he receives is stringent labor laws prohibiting the
right of boycott, of picketing, in fact, of everything,
except the right to be robbed of the fruits of his
labor.   Yet all these disastrous results of the twentieth-century fetich have taught woman nothing.   But,
then, woman will purify politics, we are assured.

Needless to say, I am not opposed to woman
suffrage on the conventional ground that she is not
equal to it.   I see neither physical, psychological,
nor mental reasons why woman should not have the
equal right to vote with man.   But that can not
possibly blind me to the absurd notion that woman
will accomplish that wherein man has failed.   If she
would not make things worse, she certainly could
not make them better.   To assume, therefore, that
she would succeed in purifying something which is
not susceptible of purification, is to credit her with
supernatural powers.   Since woman's greatest misfortune has been that she was looked upon as either

angel or devil, her true salvation lies in being placed on earth; namely, in being considered human, and therefore subject to all human follies and mistakes. Are we, then, to believe that two errors will make a right? Are we to assume that the poison already inherent in politics will be decreased, if women were to enter the political arena? The most ardent suffragists would hardly maintain such a folly.

As a matter of fact, the most advanced students of universal suffrage have come to realize that all existing systems of political power are absurd, and are completely inadequate to meet the pressing issues of life. This view is also borne out by a statement of one who is herself an ardent believer in woman suffrage, Dr. Helen L. Sumner. In her able work on *Equal Suffrage,* she says: "In Colorado, we find that equal suffrage serves to show in the most striking way the essential rottenness and degrading character of the existing system." Of course, Dr. Sumner has in mind a particular system of voting, but the same applies with equal force to the entire machinery of the representative system. With such a basis, it is difficult to understand how woman, as a political factor, would benefit either herself or the rest of mankind.

But, say our suffrage devotees, look at the countries and States where female suffrage exists. See what woman has accomplished—in Australia, New Zealand, Finland, the Scandinavian countries, and in our own four States, Idaho, Colorado, Wyoming, and Utah. Distance lends enchantment—or, to quote a

Polish formula—"it is well where we are not." Thus one would assume that those countries and States are unlike other countries or States, that they have greater freedom, greater social and economic equality, a finer appreciation of human life, deeper understanding of the great social struggle, with all the vital questions it involves for the human race.

The women of Australia and New Zealand can vote, and help make the laws. Are the labor conditions better there than they are in England, where the suffragettes are making such a heroic struggle? Does there exist a greater motherhood, happier and freer children than in England? Is woman there no longer considered a mere sex commodity? Has she emancipated herself from the Puritanical double standard of morality for men and women? Certainly none but the ordinary female stump politician will dare answer these questions in the affirmative. If that be so, it seems ridiculous to point to Australia and New Zealand as the Mecca of equal suffrage accomplishments.

On the other hand, it is a fact to those who know the real political conditions in Australia, that politics have gagged labor by enacting the most stringent labor laws, making strikes without the sanction of an arbitration committee a crime equal to treason.

Not for a moment do I mean to imply that woman suffrage is responsible for this state of affairs. I do mean, however, that there is no reason to point to Australia as a wonder-worker of woman's accomplishment, since her influence has been unable to free labor from the thraldom of political bossism.

Finland has given woman equal suffrage; nay, even the right to sit in Parliament. Has that helped to develop a greater heroism, an intenser zeal than that of the women of Russia? Finland, like Russia, smarts under the terrible whip of the bloody Tsar. Where are the Finnish Perovskaias, Spiridonovas, Figners, Breshkovskaias? Where are the countless numbers of Finnish young girls who cheerfully go to Siberia for their cause? Finland is sadly in need of heroic liberators. Why has the ballot not created them? The only Finnish avenger of his people was a man, not a woman, and he used a more effective weapon than the ballot.

As to our own States where women vote, and which are constantly being pointed out as examples of marvels, what has been accomplished there through the ballot that women do not to a large extent enjoy in other States; or that they could not achieve through energetic efforts without the ballot?

True, in the suffrage States women are guaranteed equal rights to property; but of what avail is that right to the mass of women without property, the thousands of wage workers, who live from hand to mouth? That equal suffrage did not, and cannot, affect their condition is admitted even by Dr. Sumner, who certainly is in a position to know. As an ardent suffragist, and having been sent to Colorado by the Collegiate Equal Suffrage League of New York State to collect material in favor of suffrage, she would be the last to say anything derogatory; yet we are informed that "equal suffrage has but slightly affected the economic conditions of women. That women do not receive equal pay for equal work, and that, though woman in Colorado has enjoyed school suffrage since 1876, women teachers are paid less than in California." On the other hand, Miss Sumner fails to account for the fact that although women have had school suffrage for thirty-four years, and equal suffrage since 1894, the census in Denver alone a few months ago disclosed the fact of fifteen thousand defective school children. And that, too, with mostly women in the educational department, and also notwithstanding that women in Colorado have passed the "most stringent laws for child and animal protection." The women of Colorado "have taken great interest in the State institutions for the care of dependent, defective, and delinquent children." What a horrible indictment against woman's care and interest, if one city has fifteen thousand defective children. What about the glory of woman suffrage, since it has failed utterly in the most important social issue, the child? And where is the superior sense of justice that woman was to bring into the political field? Where was it in 1903, when the mine owners waged a guerilla war against the Western Miners' Union; when General Bell established a reign of terror, pulling men out of bed at night, kidnapping them across the border line, throwing them into bull pens, declaring "to hell with the Constitution, the club is the Constitution"? Where were the women politicians then, and why did they not exercise the power of their vote? But they did. They helped to defeat the most fair-minded and liberal man, Governor Waite. The latter had to make way for the tool of the mine kings, Governor Peabody, the enemy of labor, the Tsar of Colorado. "Certainly male suffrage could have done nothing worse." Granted. Wherein, then, are the advantages to woman and society from woman suffrage? The oft-repeated assertion that woman will purify politics is also but a myth. It is not borne out by the people who know the political conditions of Idaho, Colorado, Wyoming, and Utah.

Woman, essentially a purist, is naturally bigoted and relentless in her effort to make others as good as she thinks they ought to be. Thus, in Idaho, she has disfranchised her sister of the street, and declared all women of "lewd character" unfit to vote. "Lewd" not being interpreted, of course, as prostitution *in* marriage. It goes without saying that illegal prostitution and gambling have been prohibited. In this regard the law must needs be of feminine gender: it always prohibits. Therein all laws are wonderful. They go no further, but their very tendencies open all the floodgates of hell. Prostitution and gambling have never done a more flourishing business than since the law has been set against them.

In Colorado, the Puritanism of woman has expressed itself in a more drastic form. "Men of notoriously unclean lives, and men connected with saloons, have been dropped from politics since women have the vote."* Could Brother Comstock do more?

---

* *Equal Suffrage,* Dr. Helen Sumner.

Could all the Puritan fathers have done more? I wonder how many women realize the gravity of this would-be feat. I wonder if they understand that it is the very thing which, instead of elevating woman, has made her a political spy, a contemptible pry into the private affairs of people, not so much for the good of the cause, but because, as a Colorado woman said, "they like to get into houses they have never been in, and find out all they can, politically and otherwise."* Yes, and into the human soul and its minutest nooks and corners. For nothing satisfies the craving of most women so much as scandal. And when did she ever enjoy such opportunities as are hers, the politician's?

"Notoriously unclean lives, and men connected with the saloons." Certainly, the lady vote gatherers can not be accused of much sense of proportion. Granting even that these busybodies can decide whose lives are clean enough for that eminently clean atmosphere, politics, must it follow that saloon-keepers belong to the same category? Unless it be American hypocrisy and bigotry, so manifest in the principle of Prohibition, which sanctions the spread of drunkenness among men and women of the rich class, yet keeps vigilant watch on the only place left to the poor man. If no other reason, woman's narrow and purist attitude toward life makes her a greater danger to liberty wherever she has political power. Man has long overcome the superstitions that still engulf woman. In the economic competitive field,

*Equal Suffrage.

man has been compelled to exercise efficiency, judgment, ability, competency. He therefore had neither time nor inclination to measure everyone's morality with a Puritanic yardstick. In his political activities, too, he has not gone about blindfolded. He knows that quantity and not quality is the material for the political grinding mill, and, unless he is a sentimental reformer or an old fossil, he knows that politics can never be anything but a swamp.

Women who are at all conversant with the process of politics, know the nature of the beast, but in their self-sufficiency and egotism they make themselves believe that they have but to pet the beast, and he will become as gentle as a lamb, sweet and pure. As if women have not sold their votes, as if women politicians cannot be bought! If her body can be bought in return for material consideration, why not her vote? That it is being done in Colorado and in other States, is not denied even by those in favor of woman suffrage.

As I have said before, woman's narrow view of human affairs is not the only argument against her as a politician superior to man. There are others. Her life-long economic parasitism has utterly blurred her conception of the meaning of equality. She clamors for equal rights with man, yet we learn that "few women care to canvas in undesirable districts."* How little equality means to them compared with the Russian women, who face hell itself for their ideal! Woman demands the same rights as man, yet

---

* Dr. Helen A. Sumner.

she is indignant that her presence does not strike him dead: he smokes, keeps his hat on, and does not jump from his seat like a flunkey. These may be trivial things, but they are nevertheless the key to the nature of American suffragists. To be sure, their English sisters have outgrown these silly notions. They have shown themselves equal to the greatest demands on their character and power of endurance. All honor to the heroism and sturdiness of the English suffragettes. Thanks to their energetic, aggressive methods, they have proved an inspiration to some of our own lifeless and spineless ladies. But after all, the suffragettes, too, are still lacking in appreciation of real equality. Else how is one to account for the tremendous, truly gigantic effort set in motion by those valiant fighters for a wretched little bill which will benefit a handful of propertied ladies, with absolutely no provision for the vast mass of working-women? True, as politicians they must be opportunists, must take half-measures if they can not get all. But as intelligent and liberal women they ought to realize that if the ballot is a weapon, the disinherited need it more than the economically superior class, and that the latter already enjoy too much power by virtue of their economic superiority.

The brilliant leader of the English suffragettes, Mrs. Emmeline Pankhurst, herself admitted, when on her American lecture tour, that there can be no equality between political superiors and inferiors. If so, how will the workingwomen of England, already inferior economically to the ladies who are benefited

by the Shackleton bill,* be able to work with their
political superiors, should the bill pass? Is it not
probable that the class of Annie Keeney, so full of
zeal, devotion, and martyrdom, will be compelled to
carry on their backs their female political bosses,
even as they are carrying their economic masters.
They would still have to do it, were universal suffrage for men and women established in England.
No matter what the workers do, they are made to
pay, always. Still, those who believe in the power
of the vote show little sense of justice when they
concern themselves not at all with those whom, as
they claim, it might serve most.

The American suffrage movement has been, until
very recently, altogether a parlor affair, absolutely
detached from the economic needs of the people.
Thus Susan B. Anthony, no doubt an exceptional
type of woman, was not only indifferent but antagonistic to labor; nor did she hesitate to manifest her
antagonism when, in 1869, she advised women to
take the places of striking printers in New York.†
I do not know whether her attitude had changed
before her death.

There are, of course, some suffragists who are
affiliated with workingwomen—the Women's Trade
Union League, for instance; but they are a small
minority, and their activities are essentially economic.
The rest look upon toil as a just provision of Provi-

---

* Mr. Shackleton was a labor leader. It is therefore self-
evident that he should introduce a bill excluding his own con-
stituents. The English Parliament is full of such Judases.

† *Equal Suffrage,* Dr. Helen A. Sumner.

dence. What would become of the rich, if not for the poor? What would become of these idle, parasitic ladies, who squander more in a week than their victims earn in a year, if not for the eighty million wage-workers? Equality, who ever heard of such a thing?

Few countries have produced such arrogance and snobbishness as America. Particularly is this true of the American woman of the middle class. She not only considers herself the equal of man, but his superior, especially in her purity, goodness, and morality. Small wonder that the American suffragist claims for her vote the most miraculous powers. In her exalted conceit she does not see how truly enslaved she is, not so much by man, as by her own silly notions and traditions. Suffrage can not ameliorate that sad fact; it can only accentuate it, as indeed it does.

One of the great American women leaders claims that woman is entitled not only to equal pay, but that she ought to be legally entitled even to the pay of her husband. Failing to support her, he should be put in convict stripes, and his earnings in prison be collected by his equal wife. Does not another brilliant exponent of the cause claim for woman that her vote will abolish the social evil, which has been fought in vain by the collective efforts of the most illustrious minds the world over? It is indeed to be regretted that the alleged creator of the universe has already presented us with his wonderful scheme of things, else woman suffrage would surely enable woman to outdo him completely.

Nothing is so dangerous as the dissection of a

fetich. If we have outlived the time when such heresy was punishable by the stake, we have not outlived the narrow spirit of condemnation of those who dare differ with accepted notions. Therefore I shall probably be put down as an opponent of woman. But that can not deter me from looking the question squarely in the face. I repeat what I have said in the beginning: I do not believe that woman will make politics worse; nor can I believe that she could make it better. If, then, she cannot improve on man's mistakes, why perpetrate the latter?

History may be a compilation of lies; nevertheless, it contains a few truths, and they are the only guide we have for the future. The history of the political activities of men proves that they have given him absolutely nothing that he could not have achieved in a more direct, less costly, and more lasting manner. As a matter of fact, every inch of ground he has gained has been through a constant fight, a ceaseless struggle for self-assertion, and not through suffrage. There is no reason whatever to assume that woman, in her climb to emancipation, has been, or will be, helped by the ballot.

In the darkest of all countries, Russia, with her absolute despotism, woman has become man's equal, not through the ballot, but by her will to be and to do. Not only has she conquered for herself every avenue of learning and vocation, but she has won man's esteem, his respect, his comradeship; aye, even more than that: she has gained the admiration, the respect of the whole world. That, too, not through suffrage, but by her wonderful heroism, her fortitude, her ability, willpower, and her endurance in her struggle for liberty. Where are the women in any suffrage country or State that can lay claim to such a victory? When we consider the accomplishments of woman in America, we find also that something deeper and more powerful than suffrage has helped her in the march to emancipation.

It is just sixty-two years ago since a handful of women at the Seneca Falls Convention set forth a few demands for their right to equal education with men, and access to the various professions, trades, etc. What wonderful accomplishments, what wonderful triumphs! Who but the most ignorant dare speak of woman as a mere domestic drudge? Who dare suggest that this or that profession should not be open to her? For over sixty years she has molded a new atmosphere and a new life for herself. She has become a world-power in every domain of human thought and activity. And all that without suffrage, without the right to make laws, without the "privilege" of becoming a judge, a jailer, or an executioner.

Yes, I may be considered an enemy of woman; but if I can help her see the light, I shall not complain.

The misfortune of woman is not that she is unable to do the work of a man, but that she is wasting her life-force to outdo him, with a tradition of centuries which has left her physically incapable of keeping pace with him. Oh, I know some have succeeded, but at what cost, at what terrific cost! The import is not the kind of work woman does, but rather the quality of the work she furnishes. She can give suffrage or the ballot no new quality, nor can she receive anything from it that will enhance her own quality. Her development, her freedom, her independence, must come from and through herself. First, by asserting herself as a personality, and not as a sex commodity. Second, by refusing the right to anyone over her body; by refusing to bear children, unless she wants them; by refusing to be a servant to God, the State, society, the husband, the family, etc., by making her life simpler, but deeper and richer. That is, by trying to learn the meaning and substance of life in all its complexities, by freeing herself from the fear of public opinion and public condemnation. Only that, and not the ballot, will set woman free, will make her a force hitherto unknown in the world, a force for real love, for peace, for harmony; a force of divine fire, of life-giving; a creator of free men and women.

THE TRAGEDY OF WOMAN'S
EMANCIPATION

I BEGIN with an admission: Regardless of all political
and economic theories, treating of the fundamental
differences between various groups within the human
race, regardless of class and race distinctions, regardless of all artificial boundary lines between woman's
rights and man's rights, I hold that there is a point
where these differentiations may meet and grow into
one perfect whole.

With this I do not mean to propose a peace treaty.
The general social antagonism which has taken hold
of our entire public life today, brought about through
the force of opposing and contradictory interests, will
crumble to pieces when the reorganization of our
social life, based upon the principles of economic
justice, shall have become a reality.

Peace or harmony between the sexes and individuals does not necessarily depend on a superficial
equalization of human beings; nor does it call for the
elimination of individual traits and peculiarities. The
problem that confronts us today, and which the nearest future is to solve, is how to be one's self and yet

in oneness with others, to feel deeply with all human beings and still retain one's own characteristic qualities. This seems to me to be the basis upon which the mass and the individual, the true democrat and the true individuality, man and woman, can meet without antagonism and opposition. The motto should not be: Forgive one another; rather, Understand one another. The oft-quoted sentence of Madame de Staël: "To understand everything means to forgive everything," has never particularly appealed to me; it has the odor of the confessional; to forgive one's fellow-being conveys the idea of pharisaical superiority. To understand one's fellow-being suffices. The admission partly represents the fundamental aspect of my views on the emancipation of woman and its effect upon the entire sex.

Emancipation should make it possible for woman to be human in the truest sense. Everything within her that craves assertion and activity should reach its fullest expression; all artificial barriers should be broken, and the road towards greater freedom cleared of every trace of centuries of submission and slavery.

This was the original aim of the movement for woman's emancipation. But the results so far achieved have isolated woman and have robbed her of the fountain springs of that happiness which is so essential to her. Merely external emancipation has made of the modern woman an artificial being, who reminds one of the products of French arboriculture with its arabesque trees and shrubs, pyramids, wheels, and wreaths; anything, except the forms which would be reached by the expression of her own inner quali-

ties. Such artificially grown plants of the female sex
are to be found in large numbers, especially in the
so-called intellectual sphere of our life.

Liberty and equality for woman! What hopes
and aspirations these words awakened when they
were first uttered by some of the noblest and bravest
souls of those days. The sun in all his light and
glory was to rise upon a new world; in this world
woman was to be free to direct her own destiny—
an aim certainly worthy of the great enthusiasm,
courage, perseverance, and ceaseless effort of the tremendous host of pioneer men and women, who staked
everything against a world of prejudice and ignorance.

My hopes also move towards that goal, but I hold
that the emancipation of woman, as interpreted and
practically applied today, has failed to reach that
great end. Now, woman is confronted with the
necessity of emancipating herself from emancipation,
if she really desires to be free. This may sound
paradoxical, but is, nevertheless, only too true.

What has she achieved through her emancipation?
Equal suffrage in a few States. Has that purified our
political life, as many well-meaning advocates pre-
dicted? Certainly not. Incidentally, it is really time
that persons with plain, sound judgment should cease
to talk about corruption in politics in a boarding-
school tone. Corruption of politics has nothing to do
with the morals, or the laxity of morals, of various
political personalities. Its cause is altogether a
material one. Politics is the reflex of the business and
industrial world, the mottos of which are: "To take
is more blessed than to give"; "buy cheap and sell

dear"; "one soiled hand washes the other." There is
no hope even that woman, with her right to vote, will
ever purify politics.

Emancipation has brought woman economic equality with man; that is, she can choose her own profession and trade; but as her past and present physical
training has not equipped her with the necessary
strength to compete with man, she is often compelled
to exhaust all her energy, use up her vitality, and
strain every nerve in order to reach the market value.
Very few ever succeed, for it is a fact that women
teachers, doctors, lawyers, architects, and engineers
are neither met with the same confidence as their
male colleagues, nor receive equal remuneration.
And those that do reach that enticing equality, generally do so at the expense of their physical and
psychical well-being. As to the great mass of working girls and women, how much independence is
gained if the narrowness and lack of freedom of the
home is exchanged for the narrowness and lack of
freedom of the factory, sweat-shop, department store,
or office? In addition is the burden which is laid on
many women of looking after a "home, sweet home"
—cold, dreary, disorderly, uninviting—after a day's
hard work. Glorious independence! No wonder that
hundreds of girls are so willing to accept the first offer
of marriage, sick and tired of their "independence"
behind the counter, at the sewing or typewriting
machine. They are just as ready to marry as girls of
the middle class, who long to throw off the yoke of
parental supremacy. A so-called independence which
leads only to earning the merest subsistence is not so

enticing, not so ideal, that one could expect woman to sacrifice everything for it. Our highly praised independence is, after all, but a slow process of dulling and stifling woman's nature, her love instinct, and her mother instinct.

Nevertheless, the position of the working girl is far more natural and human than that of her seemingly more fortunate sister in the more cultured professional walks of life—teachers, physicians, lawyers, engineers, etc., who have to make a dignified, proper appearance, while the inner life is growing empty and dead.

The narrowness of the existing conception of woman's independence and emancipation; the dread of love for a man who is not her social equal; the fear that love will rob her of her freedom and independence; the horror that love or the joy of motherhood will only hinder her in the full exercise of her profession—all these together make of the emancipated modern woman a compulsory vestal, before whom life, with its great clarifying sorrows and its deep, entrancing joys, rolls on without touching or gripping her soul.

Emancipation, as understood by the majority of its adherents and exponents, is of too narrow a scope to permit the boundless love and ecstasy contained in the deep emotion of the true woman, sweetheart, mother, in freedom.

The tragedy of the self-supporting or economically free woman does not lie in too many, but in too few experiences. True, she surpasses her sister of past generations in knowledge of the world and human nature; it is just because of this that she feels deeply the lack of life's essence, which alone can enrich the human soul, and without which the majority of women have become mere professional automatons.

That such a state of affairs was bound to come was foreseen by those who realized that, in the domain of ethics, there still remained many decaying ruins of the time of the undisputed superiority of man; ruins that are still considered useful. And, what is more important, a goodly number of the emancipated are unable to get along without them. Every movement that aims at the destruction of existing institutions and the replacement thereof with something more advanced, more perfect, has followers who in theory stand for the most radical ideas, but who, nevertheless, in their every-day practice, are like the average Philistine, feigning respectability and clamoring for the good opinion of their opponents. There are, for example, Socialists, and even Anarchists, who stand for the idea that property is robbery, yet who will grow indignant if anyone owe them the value of a half-dozen pins.

The same Philistine can be found in the movement for woman's emancipation. Yellow journalists and milk-and-water litterateurs have painted pictures of the emancipated woman that make the hair of the good citizen and his dull companion stand up on end. Every member of the woman's rights movement was pictured as a George Sand in her absolute disregard of morality. Nothing was sacred to her. She had no respect for the ideal relation between man and woman. In short, emancipation stood only for a reckless life of lust and sin; regardless of society, religion, and morality. The exponents of woman's rights were highly indignant at such misrepresentation, and, lacking humor, they exerted all their energy to prove that they were not at all as bad as they were painted, but the very reverse. Of course, as long as woman was the slave of man, she could not be good and pure, but now that she was free and independent she would prove how good she could be and that her influence would have a purifying effect on all institutions in society. True, the movement for woman's rights has broken many old fetters, but it has also forged new ones. The great movement of *true* emancipation has not met with a great race of women who could look liberty in the face. Their narrow, Puritanical vision banished man, as a disturber and doubtful character, out of their emotional life. Man was not to be tolerated at any price, except perhaps as the father of a child, since a child could not very well come to life without a father. Fortunately, the most rigid Puritans never will be strong enough to kill the innate craving for motherhood. But woman's freedom is closely allied with man's freedom, and many of my so-called emancipated sisters seem to overlook the fact that a child born in freedom needs the love and devotion of each human being about him, man as well as woman. Unfortunately, it is this narrow conception of human relations that has brought about a great tragedy in the lives of the modern man and woman.

About fifteen years ago appeared a work from the pen of the brilliant Norwegian Laura Marholm, called *Woman, a Character Study*. She was one of the first to call attention to the emptiness and narrowness of the existing conception of woman's emancipation, and its tragic effect upon the inner life of woman. In her work Laura Marholm speaks of the fate of several gifted women of international fame: the genius Eleonora Duse; the great mathematician and writer Sonya Kovalevskaia; the artist and poet-nature Marie Bashkirtzeff, who died so young. Through each description of the lives of these women of such extraordinary mentality runs a marked trail of unsatisfied craving for a full, rounded, complete, and beautiful life, and the unrest and loneliness resulting from the lack of it. Through these masterly psychological sketches one cannot help but see that the higher the mental development of woman, the less possible it is for her to meet a congenial mate who will see in her, not only sex, but also the human being, the friend, the comrade and strong individuality, who cannot and ought not lose a single trait of her character.

The average man with his self-sufficiency, his ridiculously superior airs of patronage towards the female sex, is an impossibility for woman as depicted in the *Character Study* by Laura Marholm. Equally impossible for her is the man who can see in her nothing more than her mentality and her genius, and who fails to awaken her woman nature.

A rich intellect and a fine soul are usually considered necessary attributes of a deep and beautiful personality. In the case of the modern woman, these attributes serve as a hindrance to the complete assertion of her being. For over a hundred years the old form of marriage, based on the Bible, "till death doth part," has been denounced as an institution that stands for the sovereignty of the man over the woman, of her complete submission to his whims and commands, and absolute dependence on his name and support. Time and again it has been conclusively proved that the old matrimonial relation restricted woman to the function of man's servant and the bearer of his children. And yet we find many emancipated women who prefer marriage, with all its deficiencies, to the narrowness of an unmarried life; narrow and unendurable because of the chains of moral and social prejudice that cramp and bind her nature.

The explanation of such inconsistency on the part of many advanced women is to be found in the fact that they never truly understood the meaning of emancipation. They thought that all that was needed was independence from external tyrannies; the internal tyrants, far more harmful to life and growth—ethical and social conventions—were left to take care of themselves; and they have taken care of themselves. They seem to get along as beautifully in the heads and hearts of the most active exponents of woman's emancipation, as in the heads and hearts of our grandmothers.

These internal tyrants, whether they be in the form of public opinion or what will mother say, or brother, father, aunt, or relative of any sort; what will Mrs. Grundy, Mr. Comstock, the employer, the Board of Education say? All these busybodies, moral detectives, jailers of the human spirit, what will they say? Until woman has learned to defy them all, to stand firmly on her own ground and to insist upon her own unrestricted freedom, to listen to the voice of her nature, whether it call for life's greatest treasure, love for a man, or her most glorious priv-ilege, the right to give birth to a child, she cannot call herself emancipated. How many emancipated women are brave enough to acknowledge that the voice of love is calling, wildly beating against their breasts, demanding to be heard, to be satisfied.

The French writer Jean Reibrach, in one of his novels, *New Beauty*, attempts to picture the ideal, beautiful, emancipated woman. This ideal is em-bodied in a young girl, a physician. She talks very cleverly and wisely of how to feed infants; she is kind, and administers medicines free to poor mothers. She converses with a young man of her acquaintance about the sanitary conditions of the future, and how various bacilli and germs shall be exterminated by the use of stone walls and floors, and by the doing away with rugs and hangings. She is, of course, very plainly and practically dressed, mostly in black. The young man, who, at their first meeting, was overawed by the wisdom of his emancipated friend, gradually learns to understand her, and recognizes one fine day that he loves her. They are young, and she is kind and beautiful, and though always in rigid attire, her appearance is softened by a spotlessly clean white collar and cuffs. One would expect that he would tell her of his love, but he is not one to commit romantic absurdities. Poetry and the enthusiasm of love cover their blushing faces before the pure beauty

of the lady. He silences the voice of his nature, and
remains correct. She, too, is always exact, always
rational, always well behaved. I fear if they had
formed a union, the young man would have risked
freezing to death. I must confess that I can see
nothing beautiful in this new beauty, who is as cold
as the stone walls and floors she dreams of. Rather
would I have the love songs of romantic ages, rather
Don Juan and Madame Venus, rather an elopement
by ladder and rope on a moonlight night, followed
by the father's curse, mother's moans, and the moral
comments of neighbors, than correctness and propriety measured by yardsticks. If love does not know
how to give and take without restrictions, it is not
love, but a transaction that never fails to lay stress on
a plus and a minus.

The greatest shortcoming of the emancipation of
the present day lies in its artificial stiffness and its
narrow respectabilities, which produce an emptiness
in woman's soul that will not let her drink from the
fountain of life. I once remarked that there seemed
to be a deeper relationship between the old-fashioned
mother and hostess, ever on the alert for the happiness of her little ones and the comfort of those she
loved, and the truly new woman, than between the
latter and her average emancipated sister. The disciples of emancipation pure and simple declared me
a heathen, fit only for the stake. Their blind zeal
did not let them see that my comparison between
the old and the new was merely to prove that a
goodly number of our grandmothers had more blood
in their veins, far more humor and wit, and certainly

a greater amount of naturalness, kind-heartedness, and simplicity, than the majority of our emancipated professional women who fill the colleges, halls of learning, and various offices. This does not mean a wish to return to the past, nor does it condemn woman to her old sphere, the kitchen and the nursery.

Salvation lies in an energetic march onward towards a brighter and clearer future. We are in need of unhampered growth out of old traditions and habits. The movement for woman's emancipation has so far made but the first step in that direction. It is to be hoped that it will gather strength to make another. The right to vote, or equal civil rights, may be good demands, but true emancipation begins neither at the polls nor in courts. It begins in woman's soul. History tells us that every oppressed class gained true liberation from its masters through its own efforts. It is necessary that woman learn that lesson, that she realize that her freedom will reach as far as her power to achieve her freedom reaches. It is, therefore, far more important for her to begin with her inner regeneration, to cut loose from the weight of prejudices, traditions, and customs. The demand for equal rights in every vocation of life is just and fair; but, after all, the most vital right is the right to love and be loved. Indeed, if partial emancipation is to become a complete and true emancipation of woman, it will have to do away with the ridiculous notion that to be loved, to be sweetheart and mother, is synonymous with being slave or subordinate. It will have to do away with the absurd notion of the dualism of the sexes, or that man and woman represent two antagonistic worlds.

Pettiness separates; breadth unites. Let us be broad and big. Let us not overlook vital things because of the bulk of trifles confronting us. A true conception of the relation of the sexes will not admit of conqueror and conquered; it knows of but one great thing: to give of one's self boundlessly, in order to find one's self richer, deeper, better. That alone can fill the emptiness, and transform the tragedy of woman's emancipation into joy, limitless joy.

MARRIAGE AND LOVE

THE popular notion about marriage and love is that they are synonymous, that they spring from the same motives, and cover the same human needs. Like most popular notions this also rests not on actual facts, but on superstition.

Marriage and love have nothing in common; they are as far apart as the poles; are, in fact, antagonistic to each other. No doubt some marriages have been the result of love. Not, however, because love could assert itself only in marriage; much rather is it because few people can completely outgrow a convention. There are to-day large numbers of men and women to whom marriage is naught but a farce, but who submit to it for the sake of public opinion. At any rate, while it is true that some marriages are based on love, and while it is equally true that in some cases love continues in married life, I maintain that it does so regardless of marriage, and not because of it.

On the other hand, it is utterly false that love results from marriage. On rare occasions one does hear of a miraculous case of a married couple falling in love after marriage, but on close examination it will be found that it is a mere adjustment to the inevitable. Certainly the growing-used to each other is far away from the spontaneity, the intensity, and beauty of love, without which the intimacy of marriage must prove degrading to both the woman and the man.

Marriage is primarily an economic arrangement, an insurance pact. It differs from the ordinary life insurance agreement only in that it is more binding, more exacting. Its returns are insignificantly small compared with the investments. In taking out an insurance policy one pays for it in dollars and cents, always at liberty to discontinue payments. If, however, woman's premium is a husband, she pays for it with her name, her privacy, her self-respect, her very life, "until death doth part." Moreover, the marriage insurance condemns her to life-long dependency, to parasitism, to complete uselessness, individual as well as social. Man, too, pays his toll, but as his sphere is wider, marriage does not limit him as much as woman. He feels his chains more in an economic sense.

Thus Dante's motto over Inferno applies with equal force to marriage: "Ye who enter here leave all hope behind."

That marriage is a failure none but the very stupid will deny. One has but to glance over the statistics of divorce to realize how bitter a failure marriage really is. Nor will the stereotyped Philistine argument that the laxity of divorce laws and the growing looseness of woman account for the fact that: first, every twelfth marriage ends in divorce; second, that since 1870 divorces have increased from

28 to 73 for every hundred thousand population; third, that adultery, since 1867, as ground for divorce, has increased 270.8 per cent.; fourth, that desertion increased 369.8 per cent.

Added to these startling figures is a vast amount of material, dramatic and literary, further elucidating this subject. Robert Herrick, in *Together;* Pinero, in *Mid-Channel;* Eugene Walter, in *Paid in Full,* and scores of other writers are discussing the barrenness, the monotony, the sordidness, the inadequacy of marriage as a factor for harmony and understanding.

The thoughtful social student will not content himself with the popular superficial excuse for this phenomenon. He will have to dig down deeper into the very life of the sexes to know why marriage proves so disastrous.

Edward Carpenter says that behind every marriage stands the life-long environment of the two sexes; an environment so different from each other that man and woman must remain strangers. Separated by an insurmountable wall of superstition, custom, and habit, marriage has not the potentiality of developing knowledge of, and respect for, each other, without which every union is doomed to failure.

Henrik Ibsen, the hater of all social shams, was probably the first to realize this great truth. Nora leaves her husband, not—as the stupid critic would have it—because she is tired of her responsibilities or feels the need of woman's rights, but because she has come to know that for eight years she had lived with a stranger and borne him children. Can there be anything more humiliating, more degrading than a life-long proximity between two strangers? No need for the woman to know anything of the man, save his income. As to the knowledge of the woman—what is there to know except that she has a pleasing appearance? We have not yet outgrown the theologic myth that woman has no soul, that she is a mere appendix to man, made out of his rib just for the convenience of the gentleman who was so strong that he was afraid of his own shadow.

Perchance the poor quality of the material whence woman comes is responsible for her inferiority. At any rate, woman has no soul—what is there to know about her? Besides, the less soul a woman has the greater her asset as a wife, the more readily will she absorb herself in her husband. It is this slavish acquiescence to man's superiority that has kept the marriage institution seemingly intact for so long a period. Now that woman is coming into her own, now that she is actually growing aware of herself as a being outside of the master's grace, the sacred institution of marriage is gradually being undermined, and no amount of sentimental lamentation can stay it.

From infancy, almost, the average girl is told that marriage is her ultimate goal; therefore her training and education must be directed towards that end. Like the mute beast fattened for slaughter, she is prepared for that. Yet, strange to say, she is allowed to know much less about her function as wife and mother than the ordinary artisan of his trade. It is indecent and filthy for a respectable girl to know anything of the marital relation. Oh, for the inconsistency of respectability, that needs the marriage vow to turn something which is filthy into the purest and most sacred arrangement that none dare question or criticize. Yet that is exactly the attitude of the average upholder of marriage. The prospective wife and mother is kept in complete ignorance of her only asset in the competitive field—sex. Thus she enters into life-long relations with a man only to find herself shocked, repelled, outraged beyond measure by the most natural and healthy instinct, sex. It is safe to say that a large percentage of the unhappiness, misery, distress, and physical suffering of matrimony is due to the criminal ignorance in sex matters that is being extolled as a great virtue. Nor is it at all an exaggeration when I say that more than one home has been broken up because of this deplorable fact.

If, however, woman is free and big enough to learn the mystery of sex without the sanction of State or Church, she will stand condemned as utterly unfit to become the wife of a "good" man, his goodness consisting of an empty head and plenty of money. Can there be anything more outrageous than the idea that a healthy, grown woman, full of life and passion, must deny nature's demand, must subdue her most intense craving, undermine her health and break her spirit, must stunt her vision, abstain from the depth and glory of sex experience until a "good" man comes along to take her unto himself as a wife? That is precisely what marriage means. How can such an arrangement end except in failure? This is one, though not the least important, factor of marriage, which differentiates it from love.

Ours is a practical age. The time when Romeo and Juliet risked the wrath of their fathers for love, when Gretchen exposed herself to the gossip of her neighbors for love, is no more. If, on rare occasions, young pople allow themselves the luxury of romance, they are taken in care by the elders, drilled and pounded until they become "sensible."

The moral lesson instilled in the girl is not whether the man has aroused her love, but rather is it, "How much?" The important and only God of practical American life: Can the man make a living? Can he support a wife? That is the only thing that justifies marriage. Gradually this saturates every thought of the girl; her dreams are not of moonlight and kisses, of laughter and tears; she dreams of shopping tours and bargain counters. This soul-poverty and sordidness are the elements inherent in the marriage institution. The State and the Church approve of no other ideal, simply because it is the one that necessitates the State and Church control of men and women.

Doubtless there are people who continue to consider love above dollars and cents. Particularly is this true of that class whom economic necessity has forced to become self-supporting. The tremendous change in woman's position, wrought by that mighty factor, is indeed phenomenal when we reflect that it is but a short time since she has entered the industrial arena. Six million women wage-earners; six million women, who have the equal right with men to be exploited, to be robbed, to go on strike; aye, to starve even. Anything more, my lord? Yes, six million wage-workers in every walk of life, from the highest brain work to the most difficult menial labor in the mines and on the railroad tracks; yes, even detectives and policemen. Surely the emancipation is complete.

Yet with all that, but a very small number of the vast army of women wage-workers look upon work as a permanent issue, in the same light as does man. No matter how decrepit the latter, he has been taught to be independent, self-supporting. Oh, I know that no one is really independent in our economic treadmill; still, the poorest specimen of a man hates to be a parasite; to be known as such, at any rate.

The woman considers her position as worker transitory, to be thrown aside for the first bidder. That is why it is infinitely harder to organize women than men. "Why should I join a union? I am going to get married, to have a home." Has she not been taught from infancy to look upon that as her ultimate calling? She learns soon enough that the home, though not so large a prison as the factory, has more solid doors and bars. It has a keeper so faithful that naught can escape him. The most tragic part, however, is that the home no longer frees her from wage-slavery; it only increases her task.

According to the latest statistics submitted before a Committee "on labor and wages, and congestion of population," ten per cent. of the wage workers in New York City alone are married, yet they must continue to work at the most poorly paid labor in the world. Add to this horrible aspect the drudgery of housework, and what remains of the protection and glory of the home? As a matter of fact, even the middle-class girl in marriage can not speak of her home, since it is the man who creates her sphere. It is not important whether the husband is a brute or a darling. What I wish to prove is that marriage guarantees woman a home only by the grace of her husband. There she moves about in *his* home, year after year, until her aspect of life and human affairs becomes as flat, narrow, and drab as her surroundings. Small wonder if she becomes a nag, petty, quarrelsome, gossipy, unbearable, thus driving the man from the house. She could not go, if she wanted to; there is no place to go. Besides, a short period of married life, of complete surrender of all faculties, absolutely incapacitates the average woman for the outside world. She becomes reckless in appearance, clumsy in her movements, dependent in her decisions, cowardly in her judgment, a weight and a bore, which most men grow to hate and despise. Wonderfully inspiring atmosphere for the bearing of life, is it not?

But the child, how is it to be protected, if not for marriage? After all, is not that the most important consideration? The sham, the hypocrisy of it! Marriage protecting the child, yet thousands of children destitute and homeless. Marriage protecting the child, yet orphan asylums and reformatories overcrowded, the Society for the Prevention of Cruelty to Children keeping busy in rescuing the little victims from "loving" parents, to place them under more loving care, the Gerry Society. Oh, the mockery of it!

Marriage may have the power to "bring the horse to water," but has it ever made him drink? The law will place the father under arrest, and put him in convict's clothes; but has that ever stilled the hunger of the child? If the parent has no work, or if he hides his identity, what does marriage do then? It invokes the law to bring the man to "justice," to put him safely behind closed doors; his labor, however, goes not to the child, but to the State. The child receives but a blighted memory of its father's stripes.

As to the protection of the woman,—therein lies the curse of marriage. Not that it really protects her, but the very idea is so revolting, such an outrage and insult on life, so degrading to human dignity, as to forever condemn this parasitic institution.

It is like that other paternal arrangement—capitalism. It robs man of his birthright, stunts his growth, poisons his body, keeps him in ignorance, in poverty and dependence, and then institutes charities that thrive on the last vestige of man's self-respect.

The institution of marriage makes a parasite of woman, an absolute dependent. It incapacitates her for life's struggle, annihilates her social consciousness, paralyzes her imagination, and then imposes its gracious protection, which is in reality a snare, a travesty on human character.

If motherhood is the highest fulfillment of woman's nature, what other protection does it need save love and freedom? Marriage but defiles, outrages, and corrupts her fulfillment. Does it not say to woman, Only when you follow me shall you bring forth life? Does it not condemn her to the block, does it not degrade and shame her if she refuses to buy her right to motherhood by selling herself? Does not marriage only sanction motherhood, even though

conceived in hatred, in compulsion? Yet, if motherhood be of free choice, of love, of ecstasy, of defiant
passion, does it not place a crown of thorns upon an
innocent head and carve in letters of blood the hideous
epithet, Bastard? Were marriage to contain all the
virtues claimed for it, its crimes against motherhood
would exclude it forever from the realm of love.

Love, the strongest and deepest element in all life,
the harbinger of hope, of joy, of ecstasy; love, the
defier of all laws, of all conventions; love, the freest,
the most powerful moulder of human destiny; how
can such an all-compelling force be synonymous with
that poor little State and Church-begotten weed,
marriage?

Free love? As if love is anything but free! Man
has bought brains, but all the millions in the world
have failed to buy love. Man has subdued bodies, but
all the power on earth has been unable to subdue love.
Man has conquered whole nations, but all his armies
could not conquer love. Man has chained and fettered the spirit, but he has been utterly helpless before
love. High on a throne, with all the splendor and
pomp his gold can command, man is yet poor and
desolate, if love passes him by. And if it stays, the
poorest hovel is radiant with warmth, with life and
color. Thus love has the magic power to make of a
beggar a king. Yes, love is free; it can dwell in no
other atmosphere. In freedom it gives itself un-
reservedly, abundantly, completely. All the laws on
the statutes, all the courts in the universe, cannot tear
it from the soil, once love has taken root. If, however, the soil is sterile, how can marriage make it bear

fruit? It is like the last desperate struggle of fleeting life against death.

Love needs no protection; it is its own protection. So long as love begets life no child is deserted, or hungry, or famished for the want of affection. I know this to be true. I know women who became mothers in freedom by the men they loved. Few children in wedlock enjoy the care, the protection, the devotion free motherhood is capable of bestowing.

The defenders of authority dread the advent of a free motherhood, lest it will rob them of their prey. Who would fight wars? Who would create wealth? Who would make the policeman, the jailer, if woman were to refuse the indiscriminate breeding of children? The race, the race! shouts the king, the president, the capitalist, the priest. The race must be preserved, though woman be degraded to a mere machine, —and the marriage institution is our only safety valve against the pernicious sex-awakening of woman. But in vain these frantic efforts to maintain a state of bondage. In vain, too, the edicts of the Church, the mad attacks of rulers, in vain even the arm of the law. Woman no longer wants to be a party to the production of a race of sickly, feeble, decrepit, wretched human beings, who have neither the strength nor moral courage to throw off the yoke of poverty and slavery. Instead she desires fewer and better children, begotten and reared in love and through free choice; not by compulsion, as marriage imposes. Our pseudo-moralists have yet to learn the deep sense of responsibility toward the child, that love in freedom has awakened in the breast of woman. Rather would she forego forever the glory of motherhood than bring forth life in an atmosphere that breathes only destruction and death. And if she does become a mother, it is to give to the child the deepest and best her being can yield. To grow with the child is her motto; she knows that in that manner alone can she help build true manhood and womanhood.

Ibsen must have had a vision of a free mother, when, with a master stroke, he portrayed Mrs. Alving. She was the ideal mother because she had outgrown marriage and all its horrors, because she had broken her chains, and set her spirit free to soar until it returned a personality, regenerated and strong. Alas, it was too late to rescue her life's joy, her Oswald; but not too late to realize that love in freedom is the only condition of a beautiful life. Those who, like Mrs. Alving, have paid with blood and tears for their spiritual awakening, repudiate marriage as an imposition, a shallow, empty mockery. They know, whether love last but one brief span of time or for eternity, it is the only creative, inspiring, elevating basis for a new race, a new world.

In our present pygmy state love is indeed a stranger to most people. Misunderstood and shunned, it rarely takes root; or if it does, it soon withers and dies. Its delicate fiber can not endure the stress and strain of the daily grind. Its soul is too complex to adjust itself to the slimy woof of our social fabric. It weeps and moans and suffers with those who have need of it, yet lack the capacity to rise to love's summit.

Some day, some day men and women will rise, they will reach the mountain peak, they will meet big and strong and free, ready to receive, to partake, and to bask in the golden rays of love. What fancy, what imagination, what poetic genius can foresee even approximately the potentialities of such a force in the life of men and women. If the world is ever to give birth to true companionship and oneness, not marriage, but love will be the parent.

THE MODERN DRAMA

So LONG as discontent and unrest make themselves but dumbly felt within a limited social class, the powers of reaction may often succeed in suppressing such manifestations. But when the dumb unrest grows into conscious expression and becomes almost universal, it necessarily affects all phases of human thought and action, and seeks its individual and social expression in the gradual transvaluation of existing values.

An adequate appreciation of the tremendous spread of the modern, conscious social unrest cannot be gained from merely propagandistic literature. Rather must we become conversant with the larger phases of human expression manifest in art, literature, and, above all, the modern drama—the strongest and most far-reaching interpreter of our deep-felt dissatisfaction.

What a tremendous factor for the awakening of conscious discontent are the simple canvasses of a Millet! The figures of his peasants—what terrific indictment against our social wrongs; wrongs that condemn the Man With the Hoe to hopeless drudgery, himself excluded from Nature's bounty.

The vision of a Meunier conceives the growing solidarity and defiance of labor in the group of miners carrying their maimed brother to safety. His genius thus powerfully portrays the interrelation of the seething unrest among those slaving in the bowels of the earth, and the spiritual revolt that seeks artistic expression.

No less important is the factor for rebellious awakening in modern literature—Turgeniev, Dostoyevsky, Tolstoy, Andreiev, Gorki, Whitman, Emerson, and scores of others embodying the spirit of universal ferment and the longing for social change.

Still more far-reaching is the modern drama, as the leaven of radical thought and the disseminator of new values.

It might seem an exaggeration to ascribe to the modern drama such an important rôle. But a study of the development of modern ideas in most countries will prove that the drama has succeeded in driving home great social truths, truths generally ignored when presented in other forms. No doubt there are exceptions, as Russia and France.

Russia, with its terrible political pressure, has made people think and has awakened their social sympathies, because of the tremendous contrast which exists between the intellectual life of the people and the despotic régime that is trying to crush that life. Yet while the great dramatic works of Tolstoy, Tchechov, Gorki, and Andreiev closely mirror the life and the struggle, the hopes and aspirations of the Russian people, they did not influence radical thought to the extent the drama has done in other countries.

Who can deny, however, the tremendous influence exerted by *The Power of Darkness* or *Night Lodging*. Tolstoy, the real, true Christian, is yet the greatest enemy of organized Christianity. With a master hand he portrays the destructive effects upon the human mind of the power of darkness, the superstitions of the Christian Church.

What other medium could express, with such dramatic force, the responsibility of the Church for crimes committed by its deluded victims; what other medium could, in consequence, rouse the indignation of man's conscience?

Similarly direct and powerful is the indictment contained in Gorki's *Night Lodging*. The social pariahs, forced into poverty and crime, yet desperately clutch at the last vestiges of hope and aspiration. Lost existences these, blighted and crushed by cruel, unsocial environment.

France, on the other hand, with her continuous struggle for liberty, is indeed the cradle of radical thought; as such she, too, did not need the drama as a means of awakening. And yet the works of Brieux —as *Robe Rouge,* portraying the terrible corruption of the judiciary—and Mirbeau's *Les Affaires sont les Affaires*—picturing the destructive influence of wealth on the human soul—have undoubtedly reached wider circles than most of the articles and books which have been written in France on the social question.

In countries like Germany, Scandinavia, England, and even in America—though in a lesser degree—the drama is the vehicle which is really making history, disseminating radical thought in ranks not otherwise to be reached.

Let us take Germany, for instance. For nearly a quarter of a century men of brains, of ideas, and of the greatest integrity, made it their life-work to spread the truth of human brotherhood, of justice, among the oppressed and downtrodden. Socialism, that tremendous revolutionary wave, was to the victims of a merciless and inhumane system like water to the parched lips of the desert traveler. Alas! The cultured people remained absolutely indifferent; to them that revolutionary tide was but the murmur of dissatisfied, discontented men, dangerous, illiterate trouble-makers, whose proper place was behind prison bars.

Self-satisfied as the "cultured" usually are, they could not understand why one should fuss about the fact that thousands of people were starving, though they contributed towards the wealth of the world. Surrounded by beauty and luxury, they could not believe that side by side with them lived human beings degraded to a position lower than a beast's, shelterless and ragged, without hope or ambition.

This condition of affairs was particularly pronounced in Germany after the Franco-German war. Full to the bursting point with its victory, Germany thrived on a sentimental, patriotic literature, thereby poisoning the minds of the country's youth by the glory of conquest and bloodshed.

Intellectual Germany had to take refuge in the literature of other countries, in the works of Ibsen, Zola, Daudet, Maupassant, and especially in the great

works of Dostoyevsky, Tolstoy, and Turgeniev. But
as no country can long maintain a standard of culture
without a literature and drama related to its own soil,
so Germany gradually began to develop a drama
reflecting the life and the struggles of its own people.

Arno Holz, one of the youngest dramatists of that
period, startled the Philistines out of their ease and
comfort with his *Familie Selicke*. The play deals
with society's refuse, men and women of the alleys,
whose only subsistence consists of what they can pick
out of the garbage barrels. A gruesome subject, is it
not? And yet what other method is there to break
through the hard shell of the minds and souls of
people who have never known want, and who therefore assume that all is well in the world?

Needless to say, ·the play aroused tremendous
indignation. The truth is bitter, and the people living
on the Fifth Avenue of Berlin hated to be confronted
with the truth.

Not that *Familie Selicke* represented anything that
had not been written about for years without any
seeming result. But the dramatic genius of Holz, together with the powerful interpretation of the play,
necessarily made inroads into the widest circles, and
forced people to think about the terrible inequalities
around them.

Sudermann's *Ehre** and *Heimat*† deal with vital
subjects. I have already referred to the sentimental
patriotism so completely turning the head of the average German as to create a perverted conception of

---

* *Honor.*
† *Magda.*

honor. Duelling became an every-day affair, costing innumerable lives. A great cry was raised against the fad by a number of leading writers. But nothing acted as such a clarifier and exposer of that national disease as the *Ehre*.

Not that the play merely deals with duelling; it analyzes the real meaning of honor, proving that it is not a fixed, inborn feeling, but that it varies with every people and every epoch, depending particularly on one's economic and social station in life. We realize from this play that the man in the brownstone mansion will necessarily define honor differently from his victims.

The family Heinecke enjoys the charity of the millionaire Mühling, being permitted to occupy a dilapidated shanty on his premises in the absence of their son, Robert. The latter, as Mühling's representative, is making a vast fortune for his employer in India. On his return Robert discovers that his sister had been seduced by young Mühling, whose father graciously offers to straighten matters with a check for 40,000 marks. Robert, outraged and indignant, resents the insult to his family's honor, and is forthwith dismissed from his position for impudence. Robert finally throws this accusation into the face of the philanthropist millionaire:

"We slave for you, we sacrifice our heart's blood for you, while you seduce our daughters and sisters and kindly pay for their disgrace with the gold we have earned for you. That is what you call honor."

An incidental side-light upon the conception of honor is given by Count Trast, the principal character in the *Ehre,* a man widely conversant with the customs of various climes, who relates that in his many travels he chanced across a savage tribe whose honor he mortally offended by refusing the hospitality which offered him the charms of the chieftain's wife.

The theme of *Heimat* treates of the struggle between the old and the young generations. It holds a permanent and important place in dramatic literature.

Magda, the daughter of Lieutenant-Colonel Schwartz, has committed an unpardonable sin: she refused the suitor selected by her father. For daring to disobey the parental commands she is driven from home. Magda, full of life and the spirit of liberty, goes out into the world to return to her native town, twelve years later, a celebrated singer. She consents to visit her parents on condition that they respect the privacy of her past. But her martinet father immediately begins to question her, insisting on his "paternal rights." Magda is indignant, but gradually his persistence brings to light the tragedy of her life. He learns that the respected Councillor von Keller had in his student days been Magda's lover, while she was battling for her economic and social independence. The consequence of the fleeting romance was a child, deserted by the man even before birth. The rigid military father of Magda demands as retribution from Councillor von Keller that he legalize the love affair. In view of Magda's social and professional success, Keller willingly consents, but on condition that she forsake the stage, and place the child in an institution. The struggle between the Old and the

New culminates in Magda's defiant words of the woman grown to conscious independence of thought and action: ". . . I'll say what I think of you—of you and your respectable society. Why should I be worse than you that I must prolong my existence among you by a lie! Why should this gold upon my body, and the lustre which surrounds my name, only increase my infamy? Have I not worked early and late for ten long years? Have I not woven this dress with sleepless nights? Have I not built up my career step by step, like thousands of my kind? Why should I blush before anyone? I am myself, and through myself I have become what I am."

The general theme of *Heimat*—the struggle between the old and young generations—was not original. It had been previously treated by a master hand in *Fathers and Sons,* portraying the awakening of an age. But though artistically far inferior to Turgeniev's work, *Heimat*—depicting the awakening of a sex—proved a powerful revolutionizing factor, mainly because of its dramatic expression.

The dramatist who not only disseminated radicalism, but literally revolutionized the thoughtful Germans, is Gerhardt Hauptmann. His first play, *Vor Sonnenaufgang,** refused by every leading German theatre, but finally performed in the independent Lessing Theatre, acted like a stroke of lightning, illuminating the entire social horizon. Its subject matter deals with the life of an extensive land-owner, ignorant, illiterate, and brutalized, and his economic

---

Before Sunrise.

slaves of the same mental calibre. The influence of
wealth, both on the victims who created it and the
possessor thereof, is shown in the most vivid colors,
as resulting in drunkenness, idiocy, and decay. But
the most striking feature of *Vor Sonnenaufgang,* the
one which brought a shower of abuse on Hauptmann's
head, was the question as to the indiscriminate breeding of children by unfit parents.

During the second performance of the play a leading Berlin surgeon almost caused a panic in the
theatre by swinging a pair of forceps over his head
and screaming at the top of his voice: "The decency
and morality of Germany are at stake if childbirth is
to be discussed openly from the stage." The surgeon
is forgotten, and Hauptmann stands a colossal figure
before the world.

When *Die Weber** first saw the light, pande-
monium broke out in the land of thinkers and poets.
"What," cried the moralists, "workingmen, dirty,
filthy slaves, to be put on the stage! Poverty in all
its horrors and ugliness to be dished out as an after-
dinner amusement? That is too much!"

Indeed, it was too much for the fat and greasy
bourgeoisie to be brought face to face with the horrors
of the weaver's existence. It was too much because
of the truth and reality that rang like thunder in the
deaf ears of self-satisfied society, *J'accuse!*

Of course, it was generally known even before the
appearance of this drama that capital can not get fat
unless it devours labor, that wealth can not be hoarded

---

* *The Weavers.*

except through the channels of poverty, hunger, and cold; but such things are better kept in the dark, lest the victims awaken to a realization of their position. But it is the purpose of the modern drama to rouse the consciousness of the oppressed; and that, indeed, was the purpose of Gerhardt Hauptmann in depicting to the world the conditions of the weavers in Silesia. Human beings working eighteen hours daily, yet not earning enough for bread and fuel; human beings living in broken, wretched huts half covered with snow, and nothing but tatters to protect them from the cold; infants covered with scurvy from hunger and exposure; pregnant women in the last stages of consumption. Victims of a benevolent Christian era, without life, without hope, without warmth. Ah, yes, it was too much!

Hauptmann's dramatic versatility deals with every stratum of social life. Besides portraying the grinding effect of economic conditions, he also treats of the struggle of the individual for his mental and spiritual liberation from the slavery of convention and tradition. Thus Heinrich, the bell-forger, in the dramatic prose-poem *Die Versunkene Glocke*,* fails to reach the mountain peaks of liberty because, as Rautende-lein said, he had lived in the valley too long. Similarly Dr. Vockerath and Anna Maar remain lonely souls because they, too, lack the strength to defy venerated traditions. Yet their very failure must awaken the rebellious spirit against a world forever hindering individual and social emancipation.

---

* *The Sunken Bell.*

Max Halbe's *Jugend** and Wedekind's *Frühling's Erwachen†* are dramas which have disseminated radical thought in an altogether different direction. They treat of the child and the dense ignorance and narrow Puritanism that meet the awakening of nature. Particularly is this true of *Frühling's Erwachen*. Young girls and boys sacrificed on the altar of false education and of our sickening morality that prohibits the enlightenment of youth as to questions so imperative to the health and well-being of society,— the origin of life, and its functions. It shows how a mother—and a truly good mother, at that—keeps her fourteen-year-old daughter in absolute ignorance as to all matters of sex, and when finally the young girl falls a victim to her ignorance, the same mother sees her child killed by quack medicines. The inscription on her grave states that she died of anaemia, and morality is satisfied.

The fatality of our Puritanic hypocrisy in these matters is especially illumined by Wedekind in so far as our most promising children fall victims to sex ignorance and the utter lack of appreciation on the part of the teachers of the child's awakening.

Wendla, unusually developed and alert for her age, pleads with her mother to explain the mystery of life:

"I have a sister who has been married for two and a half years. I myself have been made an aunt for the third time, and I haven't the least idea how it all comes about. . . . Don't be cross, Mother, dear! Whom in the world should I ask but you? Don't

---

* *Youth.*
† *The Awakening of Spring.*

scold me for asking about it. Give me an answer.—
How does it happen?—You cannot really deceive
yourself that I, who am fourteen years old, still
believe in the stork."

Were her mother herself not a victim of false
notions of morality, an affectionate and sensible
explanation might have saved her daughter. But the
conventional mother seeks to hide her "moral" shame
and embarrassment in this evasive reply:

"In order to have a child—one must love—the
man—to whom one is married. . . . One must love
him, Wendla, as you at your age are still unable to
love.—Now you know it!"

How much Wendla "knew" the mother realized
too late. The pregnant girl imagines herself ill with
dropsy. And when her mother cries in desperation,
"You haven't the dropsy, you have a child, girl," the
agonized Wendla exclaims in bewilderment: "But it's
not possible, Mother, I am not married yet. . . . Oh,
Mother, why didn't you tell me everything?"

With equal stupidity the boy Morris is driven to
suicide because he fails in his school examinations
And Melchior, the youthful father of Wendla's unborn
child, is sent to the House of Correction, his early
sexual awakening stamping him a degenerate in the
eyes of teachers and parents.

For years thoughtful men and women in Germany
had advocated the compelling necessity of sex enlightenment. *Mutterschutz,* a publication specially devoted
to frank and intelligent discussion of the sex problem,
has been carrying on its agitation for a considerable
time. But it remained for the dramatic genius of

Wedekind to influence radical thought to the extent
of forcing the introduction of sex physiology in many
schools of Germany.

Scandinavia, like Germany, was advanced through
the drama much more than through any other channel. Long before Ibsen appeared on the scene, Björnson, the great essayist, thundered against the inequalities and injustice prevalent in those countries. But his
was a voice in the wilderness, reaching but the few.
Not so with Ibsen. His *Brand, Doll's House, Pillars
of Society, Ghosts,* and *An Enemy of the People* have
considerably undermined the old conceptions, and
replaced them by a modern and real view of life. One
has but to read *Brand* to realize the modern conception, let us say, of religion,—religion, as an ideal to be
achieved on earth; religion as a principle of human
brotherhood, of solidarity, and kindness.

Ibsen, the supreme hater of all social shams, has
torn the veil of hypocrisy from their faces. His
greatest onslaught, however, is on the four cardinal
points supporting the flimsy network of society.
First, the lie upon which rests the life of today;
second, the futility of sacrifice as preached by our
moral codes; third, petty material consideration, which
is the only god the majority worships; and fourth, the
deadening influence of provincialism. These four
recur as the *Leitmotiv* in most of Ibsen's plays, but
particularly in *Pillars of Society, Doll's House,
Ghosts,* and *An Enemy of the People.*

Pillars of Society! What a tremendous indictment
against the social structure that rests on rotten and
decayed pillars,—pillars nicely gilded and apparently

intact, yet merely hiding their true condition. And what are these pillars?

Consul Bernick, at the very height of his social and financial career, the benefactor of his town and the strongest pillar of the community, has reached the summit through the channel of lies, deception, and fraud. He has robbed his bosom friend Johann of his good name, and has betrayed Lona Hessel, the woman he loved, to marry her stepsister for the sake of her money. He has enriched himself by shady transactions, under cover of "the community's good," and finally even goes to the extent of endangering human life by preparing the *Indian Girl,* a rotten and dangerous vessel, to go to sea.

But the return of Lona brings him the realization of the emptiness and meanness of his narrow life. He seeks to placate the waking conscience by the hope that he has cleared the ground for the better life of his son, of the new generation. But even this last hope soon falls to the ground, as he realizes that truth cannot be built on a lie. At the very moment when the whole town is prepared to celebrate the great benefactor of the community with banquet praise, he himself, now grown to full spiritual manhood, confesses to the assembled townspeople:

"I have no right to this homage—. . . My fellow-citizens must know me to the core. Then let everyone examine himself, and let us realize the prediction that from this event we begin a new time. The old, with its tinsel, its hypocrisy, its hollowness, its lying propriety, and its pitiful cowardice, shall lie behind us like a museum, open for instruction."

With a *Doll's House* Ibsen has paved the way for woman's emancipation. Nora awakens from her doll's rôle to the realization of the injustice done her by her father and her husband, Helmer Torvald.

"While I was at home with father, he used to tell me all his opinions, and I held the same opinions. If I had others I concealed them, because he would not have approved. He used to call me his doll child, and play with me as I played with my dolls. Then I came to live in your house. You settled everything according to your taste, and I got the same taste as you, or I pretended to. When I look back on it now, I seem to have been living like a beggar, from hand to mouth. I lived by performing tricks for you, Torvald, but you would have it so. You and father have done me a great wrong."

In vain Helmer uses the old philistine arguments of wifely duty and social obligations. Nora has grown out of her doll's dress into full stature of conscious womanhood. She is determined to think and judge for herself. She has realized that, before all else, she is a human being, owing the first duty to herself. She is undaunted even by the possibility of social ostracism. She has become sceptical of the justice of the law, the wisdom of the constituted. Her rebelling soul rises in protest against the existing. In her own words: "I must make up my mind which is right, society or I."

In her childlike faith in her husband she had hoped for the great miracle. But it was not the disappointed hope that opened her vision to the falsehoods of marriage. It was rather the smug contentment of Helmer with a safe lie—one that would remain hidden and not endanger his social standing.

When Nora closed behind her the door of her gilded cage and went out into the world a new, regenerated personality, she opened the gate of freedom and truth for her own sex and the race to come.

More than any other play, *Ghosts* has acted like a bomb explosion, shaking the social structure to its very foundations.

In *Doll's House* the justification of the union between Nora and Helmer rested at least on the husband's conception of integrity and rigid adherence to our social morality.   Indeed, he was the conventional ideal husband and devoted father.   Not so in *Ghosts*. Mrs. Alving married Captain Alving only to find that he was a physical and mental wreck, and that life with him would mean utter degradation and be fatal to possible offspring.   In her despair she turned to her youth's companion, young Pastor Manders who, as the true savior of souls for heaven, must needs be indifferent to earthly necessities.   He sent her back to shame and degradation,—to her duties to husband and home.   Indeed, happiness—to him—was but the unholy manifestation of a rebellious spirit, and a wife's duty was not to judge, but "to bear with humility the cross which a higher power had for your own good laid upon you."

Mrs. Alving bore the cross for twenty-six long years.   Not for the sake of the higher power, but for her little son Oswald, whom she longed to save from the poisonous atmosphere of her husband's home.

It was also for the sake of the beloved son that

she supported the lie of his father's goodness, in super-
stitious awe of "duty and decency." She learned—
alas, too late—that the sacrifice of her entire life had
been in vain, and that her son Oswald was visited by
the sins of his father, that he was irrevocably doomed.
This, too, she learned, that "we are all of us ghosts.
It is not only what we have inherited from our father
and mother that walks in us. It is all sorts of dead
ideas and lifeless old beliefs. They have no vitality,
but they cling to us all the same and we can't get rid
of them. . . . And then we are, one and all, so piti-
fully afraid of light. When you forced me under the
yoke you called Duty and Obligation; when you
praised as right and proper what my whole soul
rebelled against as something loathsome, it was then
that I began to look into the seams of your doctrine. I
only wished to pick at a single knot, but when I had
got that undone, the whole thing ravelled out. And
then I understood that it was all machine-sewn."

How could a society machine-sewn, fathom the
seething depths whence issued the great masterpiece
of Henrik Ibsen? It could not understand, and therefore it poured the vials of abuse and venom upon its
greatest benefactor. That Ibsen was not daunted he
has proved by his reply in *An Enemy of the People*.

In that great drama Ibsen performs the last funeral
rites over a decaying and dying social system. Out
of its ashes rises the regenerated individual, the bold
and daring rebel. Dr. Stockman, an idealist, full of
social sympathy and solidarity, is called to his native
town as the physician of the baths. He soon discovers that the latter are built on a swamp, and that

instead of finding relief the patients, who flock to the place, are being poisoned.

An honest man, of strong convictions, the doctor considers it his duty to make his discovery known. But he soon learns that dividends and profits are concerned neither with health nor priniciples. Even the reformers of the town, represented in the *People's Messenger,* always ready to prate of their devotion to the people, withdraw their support from the "reckless" idealist, the moment they learn that the doctor's discovery may bring the town into disrepute, and thus injure their pockets.

But Doctor Stockman continues in the faith he entertains for his townsmen. They would hear him. But here, too, he soon finds himself alone. He cannot even secure a place to proclaim his great truth. And when he finally succeeds, he is overwhelmed by abuse and ridicule as the enemy of the people. The doctor, so enthusiastic of his townspeople's assistance to eradicate the evil, is soon driven to a solitary position. The announcement of his discovery would result in a pecuniary loss to the town, and that consideration induces the officials, the good citizens, and soul reformers, to stifle the voice of truth. He finds them all a compact majority, unscrupulous enough to be willing to build up the prosperity of the town on a quagmire of lies and fraud. He is accused of trying to ruin the community. But to his mind "it does not matter if a lying community is ruined. It must be levelled to the ground. All men who live upon lies must be exterminated like vermin. You'll bring it to such a pass that the whole country will deserve to perish."

Doctor Stockman is not a practical politician. A free man, he thinks, must not behave like a blackguard. "He must not so act that he would spit in his own face." For only cowards permit "considerations" of pretended general welfare or of party to override truth and ideals. "Party programmes wring the necks of all young, living truths; and considerations of expediency turn morality and righteousness upside down, until life is simply hideous."

These plays of Ibsen—*The Pillars of Society, A Doll's House, Ghosts,* and *An Enemy of the People*—constitute a dynamic force which is gradually dissipating the ghosts walking the social burying ground called civilization. Nay, more; Ibsen's destructive effects are at the same time supremely constructive, for he not merely undermines existing pillars; indeed, he builds with sure strokes the foundation of a healthier, ideal future, based on the sovereignty of the individual within a sympathetic social environment.

England with her great pioneers of radical thought, the intellectual pilgrims like Godwin, Robert Owen, Darwin, Spencer, William Morris, and scores of others; with her wonderful larks of liberty—Shelley, Byron, Keats—is another example of the influence of dramatic art. Within comparatively a few years the dramatic works of Shaw, Pinero, Galsworthy, Rann Kennedy, have carried radical thought to the ears formerly deaf even to Great Britain's wondrous poets. Thus a public which will remain indifferent reading an essay by Robert Owen on poverty, or ignore Bernard Shaw's Socialistic tracts, was made to think by *Major Barbara,* wherein poverty is described as the greatest crime of Christian civilization. "Poverty makes people weak, slavish, puny; poverty creates disease, crime, prostitution; in fine, poverty is responsible for all the ills and evils of the world." Poverty also necessitates dependency, charitable organizations, institutions that thrive off the very thing they are trying to destroy. The Salvation Army, for instance, as shown in *Major Barbara*, fights drunkenness; yet one of its greatest contributors is Badger, a whiskey distiller, who furnishes yearly thousands of pounds to do away with the very source of his wealth. Bernard Shaw therefore concludes that the only real benefactor of society is a man like Undershaft, Barbara's father, a cannon manufacturer, whose theory of life is that powder is stronger than words.

"The worst of crimes," says Undershaft, "is poverty. All the other crimes are virtues beside it; all the other dishonors are chivalry itself by comparison. Poverty blights whole cities; spreads horrible pestilences; strikes dead the very soul of all who come within sight, sound, or smell of it. What you call crime is nothing; a murder here, a theft there, a blow now and a curse there: what do they matter? They are only the accidents and illnesses of life; there are not fifty genuine professional criminals in London. But there are millions of poor people, abject people, dirty people, ill-fed, ill-clothed people. They poison us morally and physically; they kill the happiness of society; they force us to do away with our own liberties and to organize unnatural cruelties for fear they should rise against us and drag us down into their

abyss. . . . Poverty and slavery have stood up for
centuries to your sermons and leading articles; they
will not stand up to my machine guns. Don't preach
at them; don't reason with them. Kill them. . . .
It is the final test of conviction, the only lever strong
enough to overturn a social system. . . . Vote! Bah!
When you vote, you only change the name of the
cabinet. When you shoot, you pull down governments, inaugurate new epochs, abolish old orders, and
set up new."

No wonder people cared little to read Mr. Shaw's
Socialistic tracts. In no other way but in the drama
could he deliver such forcible, historic truths. And
therefore it is only through the drama that Mr. Shaw
is a revolutionary factor in the dissemination of radical ideas.

After Hauptmann's *Die Weber, Strife,* by Galsworthy, is the most important labor drama.

The theme of *Strife* is a strike with two dominant
factors: Anthony, the president of the company, rigid,
uncompromising, unwilling to make the slightest con-
cession, although the men held out for months and are
in a condition of semi-starvation; and David Roberts,
an uncompromising revolutionist, whose devotion to
the workingmen and the cause of freedom is at white
heat. Between them the strikers are worn and weary
with the terrible struggle, and are harassed and
driven by the awful sight of poverty and want in their
families.

The most marvelous and brilliant piece of work in
Strife is Galsworthy's portrayal of the mob in its
fickleness and lack of backbone. One moment they

applaud old Thomas, who speaks of the power of God and religion and admonishes the men against rebellion; the next instant they are carried away by a walking delegate, who pleads the cause of the union,—the union that always stands for compromise, and which forsakes the workingmen whenever they dare to strike for independent demands; again they are aglow with the earnestness, the spirit, and the intensity of David Roberts—all these people willing to go in whatever direction the wind blows. It is the curse of the working class that they always follow like sheep led to slaughter.

Consistency is the greatest crime of our commercial age. No matter how intense the spirit or how important the man, the moment he will not allow himself to be used or sell his principles, he is thrown on the dustheap. Such was the fate of the president of the company, Anthony, and of David Roberts. To be sure they represented opposite poles—poles antagonistic to each other, poles divided by a terrible gap that can never be bridged over. Yet they shared a common fate. Anthony is the embodiment of conservatism, of old ideas, of iron methods:

"I have been chairman of this company thirty-two years. I have fought the men four times. I have never been defeated. It has been said that times have changed. If they have, I have not changed with them. It has been said that masters and men are equal. Cant. There can be only one master in a house. It has been said that Capital and Labor have the same interests. Cant. Their interests are as wide asunder as the poles. There is only one way of treating men—

with the iron rod. Masters are masters. Men are men."

We may not like this adherence to old, reactionary notions, and yet there is something admirable in the courage and consistency of this man, nor is he half as dangerous to the interests of the oppressed, as our sentimental and soft reformers who rob with nine fingers, and give libraries with the tenth; who grind human beings like Russell Sage, and then spend millions of dollars in social research work; who turn beautiful young plants into faded old women, and then give them a few paltry dollars or found a Home for Working Girls. Anthony is a worthy foe; and to fight such a foe, one must learn to meet him in open battle.

David Roberts has all the mental and moral attributes of his adversary, coupled with the spirit of revolt and the depth of modern ideas. He, too, is consistent, and wants nothing for his class short of complete victory.

"It is not for this little moment of time we are fighting, not for our own little bodies and their warmth: it is for all those who come after, for all times. Oh, men, for the love of them don't turn up another stone on their heads, don't help to blacken the sky. If we can shake that white-faced monster with the bloody lips that has sucked the lives out of ourselves, our wives, and children, since the world began, if we have not the hearts of men to stand against it, breast to breast and eye to eye, and force it backward till it cry for mercy, it will go on sucking life, and we shall stay forever where we are, less than the very dogs."

It is inevitable that compromise and petty interest should pass on and leave two such giants behind. Inevitable, until the mass will reach the stature of a David Roberts. Will it ever? Prophecy is not the vocation of the dramatist, yet the moral lesson is evident. One cannot help realizing that the workingmen will have to use methods hitherto unfamiliar to them; that they will have to discard all those elements in their midst that are forever ready to reconcile the irreconcilable, namely Capital and Labor. They will have to learn that characters like David Roberts are the very forces that have revolutionized the world and thus paved the way for emancipation out of the clutches of that "white-faced monster with bloody lips," towards a brighter horizon, a freer life, and a deeper recognition of human values.

No subject of equal social import has received such extensive consideration within the last few years as the question of prison and punishment.

Hardly any magazine of consequence that has not devoted its columns to the discussion of this vital theme. A number of books by able writers, both in America and abroad, have discussed this topic from the historic, psychologic, and social standpoint, all agreeing that present penal institutions and our mode of coping with crime have in every respect proved inadequate as well as wasteful. One would expect that something very radical should result from the cumulative literary indictment of the social crimes perpetrated upon the prisoner. Yet with the exception of a few minor and comparatively insignificant reforms in some of our prisons, absolutely nothing has been accomplished. But at last this grave social wrong has found dramatic interpretation in Galsworthy's *Justice*.

The play opens in the office of James How and Sons, Solicitors. The senior clerk, Robert Cokeson, discovers that a check he had issued for nine pounds has been forged to ninety. By elimination, suspicion falls upon William Falder, the junior office clerk. The latter is in love with a married woman, the abused, ill-treated wife of a brutal drunkard. Pressed by his employer, a severe yet not unkindly man, Falder confesses the forgery, pleading the dire necessity of his sweetheart, Ruth Honeywill, with whom he had planned to escape to save her from the unbearable brutality of her husband. Notwithstanding the entreaties of young Walter, who is touched by modern ideas, his father, a moral and law-respecting citizen, turns Falder over to the police.

The second act, in the court-room, shows Justice in the very process of manufacture. The scene equals in dramatic power and psychologic verity the great court scene in *Resurrection*. Young Falder, a nervous and rather weakly youth of twenty-three, stands before the bar. Ruth, his married sweetheart, full of love and devotion, burns with anxiety to save the youth whose affection brought about his present predicament. The young man is defended by Lawyer Frome, whose speech to the jury is a masterpiece of deep social philosophy wreathed with the tendrils of human understanding and sympathy. He does not attempt to dispute the mere fact of Falder having altered the check; and though he pleads temporary aberration in defense of his client, that plea is based upon a social consciousness as deep and all-embracing as the roots of our social ills—"the background of life, that palpitating life which always lies behind the commission of a crime." He shows Falder to have faced the alternative of seeing the beloved woman murdered by her brutal husband, whom she cannot divorce; or of taking the law into his own hands. The defence pleads with the jury not to turn the weak young man into a criminal by condemning him to prison, for "justice is a machine that, when someone has given it a starting push, rolls on of itself. . . . Is this young man to be ground to pieces under this machine for an act which, at the worst, was one of weakness? Is he to become a member of the luckless crews that man those dark, ill-starred ships called prisons? . . . I urge you, gentlemen, do not ruin this young man. For as a result of those four minutes, ruin, utter and irretrievable, stares him in the face. . . . The rolling of the chariot wheels of Justice over this boy began when it was decided to prosecute him."

But the chariot of Justice rolls mercilessly on, for—as the learned Judge says—"the law is what it is—a majestic edifice, sheltering all of us, each stone of which rests on another."

Falder is sentenced to three years' penal servitude.

In prison, the young, inexperienced convict soon finds himself the victim of the terrible "system." The authorities admit that young Falder is mentally and physically "in bad shape," but nothing can be done in

the matter: many others are in a similar position, and
"the quarters are inadequate."

The third scene of the third act is heart-gripping
in its silent force. The whole scene is a pantomime,
taking place in Falder's prison cell.

"In fast-falling daylight, Falder, in his stockings,
is seen standing motionless, with his head inclined
towards the door, listening. He moves a little closer
to the door, his stockinged feet making no noise. He
stops at the door. He is trying harder and harder to
hear something, any little thing that is going on outside. He springs suddenly upright—as if at a sound
—and remains perfectly motionless. Then, with a
heavy sigh, he moves to his work, and stands looking
at it, with his head down; he does a stitch or two,
having the air of a man so lost in sadness that each
stitch is, as it were, a coming to life. Then, turning
abruptly, he begins pacing his cell, moving his head,
like an animal pacing its cage. He stops again at the
door, listens, and, placing the palms of his hands
against it with his fingers spread out, leans his forehead against the iron. Turning from it, presently, he
moves slowly back towards the window, holding his
head, as if he felt that it were going to burst, and
stops under the window. But since he cannot see out
of it he leaves off looking, and, picking up the lid of
one of the tins, peers into it, as if trying to make a
companion of his own face. It has grown very nearly
dark. Suddenly the lid falls out of his hand with
a clatter—the only sound that has broken the silence
—and he stands staring intently at the wall where
the stuff of the shirt is hanging rather white in the

darkness—he seems to be seeing somebody or something there. There is a sharp tap and click; the cell light behind the glass screen has been turned up. The cell is brightly lighted. Falder is seen gasping for breath.

"A sound from far away, as of distant, dull beating on thick metal, is suddenly audible. Falder shrinks back, not able to bear this sudden clamor. But the sound grows, as though some great tumbril were rolling towards the cell. And gradually it seems to hypnotize him. He begins creeping inch by inch nearer to the door. The banging sound, traveling from cell to cell, draws closer and closer; Falder's hands are seen moving as if his spirit had already joined in this beating, and the sound swells till it seems to have entered the very cell. He suddenly raises his clenched fists. Panting violently, he flings himself at his door, and beats on it."

Finally Falder leaves the prison, a broken ticket-of-leave man, the stamp of the convict upon his brow, the iron of misery in his soul. Thanks to Ruth's pleading, the firm of James How and Son is willing to take Falder back in their employ, on condition that he give up Ruth. It is then that Falder learns the awful news that the woman he loves had been driven by the merciless economic Moloch to sell herself. She "tried making skirts . . . cheap things. . . . I never made more than ten shillings a week, buying my own cotton, and working all day. I hardly ever got to bed till past twelve. . . . And then . . . my employer happened—he's happened ever since." At this terrible psychologic moment the

police appear to drag him back to prison for failing
to report himself as ticket-of-leave man. Completely
overcome by the inexorability of his environment,
young Falder seeks and finds peace, greater than
human justice, by throwing himself down to death, as
the detectives are taking him back to prison.

It would be impossible to estimate the effect produced by this play. Perhaps some conception can
be gained from the very unusual circumstance that
it had proved so powerful as to induce the Home Sec-
retary of Great Britain to undertake extensive prison
reforms in England. A very encouraging sign this,
of the influence exerted by the modern drama. It is
to be hoped that the thundering indictment of Mr.
Galsworthy will not remain without similar effect upon
the public sentiment and prison conditions of America.
At any rate it is certain that no other modern play
has borne such direct and immediate fruit in wakening
the social conscience.

Another modern play, *The Servant in the House*,
strikes a vital key in our social life. The hero of
Mr. Kennedy's masterpiece is Robert, a coarse, filthy
drunkard, whom respectable society has repudiated.
Robert, the sewer cleaner, is the real hero of the play;
nay, its true and only savior. It is he who volunteers
to go down into the dangerous sewer, so that his
comrades "can 'ave light and air." After all, has he
not sacrificed his life always, so that others may have
light and air?

The thought that labor is the redeemer of social
well-being has been cried from the housetops in every
tongue and every clime. Yet the simple words of

Robert express the significance of labor and its mission with far greater potency.

America is still in its dramatic infancy. Most of the attempts along this line to mirror life, have been wretched failures. Still, there are hopeful signs in the attitude of the intelligent public toward modern plays, even if they be from foreign soil.

The only real drama America has so far produced is *The Easiest Way*, by Eugene Walter.

It is supposed to represent a "peculiar phase" of New York life. If that were all, it would be of minor significance. That which gives the play its real importance and value lies much deeper. It lies, first, in the fundamental current of our social fabric which drives us all, even stronger characters than Laura, into the easiest way—a way so very destructive of integrity, truth, and justice. Secondly, the cruel, senseless fatalism conditioned in Laura's sex. These two features put the universal stamp upon the play, and characterize it as one of the strongest dramatic indictments against society.

The criminal waste of human energy, in economic and social conditions, drives Laura as it drives the average girl to marry any man for a "home"; or as it drives men to endure the worst indignities for a miserable pittance.

Then there is that other respectable institution, the fatalism of Laura's sex. The inevitability of that force is summed up in the following words: "Don't you know that we count no more in the life of these men than tamed animals? It's a game, and if we don't play our cards well, we lose." Woman in the

battle with life has but one weapon, one commodity—
sex. That alone serves as a trump card in the game
of life.

This blind fatalism has made of woman a parasite,
an inert thing. Why then expect perseverance or
energy of Laura? The easiest way is the path mapped
out for her from time immemorial. She could follow
no other.

A number of other plays could be quoted as characteristic of the growing rôle of the drama as a disseminator of radical thought. Suffice it to mention
The Third Degree, by Charles Klein; *The Fourth
Estate*, by Medill Patterson; *A Man's World*, by Ida
Croutchers,—all pointing to the dawn of dramatic art
in America, an art which is discovering to the people
the terrible diseases of our social body.

It has been said of old, all roads lead to Rome. In
paraphrased application to the tendencies of our day,
it may truly be said that all roads lead to the great
social reconstruction. The economic awakening of the
workingman, and his realization of the necessity for
concerted industrial action; the tendencies of modern
education, especially in their application to the free
development of the child; the spirit of growing unrest
expressed through, and cultivated by, art and literature, all pave the way to the Open Road. Above all,
the modern drama, operating through the double channel of dramatist and interpreter, affecting as it does
both mind and heart, is the strongest force in developing social discontent, swelling the powerful tide of
unrest that sweeps onward and over the dam of ignorance, prejudice, and superstition.

OTHER BOOKS BY
FREDERICK ELLIS

(Buy Direct at 35% off – Contact frederick659@yahoo.com)

Author - Jack London

MARTIN EDEN

WAR OF THE CLASSES

JOHN BARLEYCORN

THE PEOPLE OF THE ABYSS

JACK LONDON ON THE ROAD

THE ASSASSINATION BUREAU, LTD.

THE IRON HEEL

Author – B. Traven

GENERAL FROM THE JUNGLE

THE DEATH SHIP

THE REBELLION OF THE HANGED

THE WHITE ROSE

THE BRIDGE IN THE JUNGLE

MARCH TO THE MONTERIA

THE TREASURE OF THE SIERRA MADRE

> Author - Carl Frederick

est PLAYING THE GAME THE NEW WAY

> Authors - Frederick Ellis & Carl Frederick

THE OAKLAND STATEMENT

> Author – Mao Tsetung

QUOTATIONS FROM CHAIRMAN MAO TSETUNG

> Author – Upton Sinclair

OUR LADY

THE FLIVVER KING: THE STORY OF FORD-AMERICA

ONE HUNDRED PERCENT: THE STORY OF A PATRIOT

WORLD'S END I

WORLD'S END II

THE SECRET LIFE OF JESUS

THE MONEYCHANGERS

MENTAL RADIO

THE MILLENNIUM

A PERSONAL JESUS

PROFITS OF RELIGION

THEY CALL ME CARPENTER: A TALE OF
THE SECOND COMING

    Author – Thomas Paine

COMMON SENSE, THE RIGHTS OF MAN
& THE AGE OF REASON

THE AMERICAN CRISIS

    Author – Karl Marx

DAS KAPITAL

THE COMMUNIST MANIFESTO &
WAGES, PRICE AND PROFIT

WAGE-LABOUR AND CAPITAL
& VALUE. PRICE AND PROFIT

    Author – Eugene Debs

WALLS AND BARS

    Author – Jean-Jacques Rousseau

THE SOCIAL CONTRACT

Author – Rosa Luxemburg

REFORM OR REVOLUTION & THE MASS STRIKE

Author – John Stuart Mill

ON SOCIALISM & THE SUBJECTION OF WOMEN

Author – THE HOLY SPIRIT

THE GOOD NEWS: AS TOLD BY MATTHEW, MARK, LUKE AND JOHN

Author – John Quincy Adams

THE AMISTAD ARGUMENT & THE STATE OF THE UNION ADDRESSES